MACHIAVELLI

Cynic, Patriot, or Political Scientist?

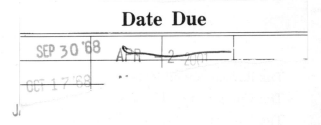

Date Due

SEP 30 '68	APR 2 2001	
OCT 17 '68		

PROBLEMS IN EUROPEAN CIVILIZATION

UNDER THE EDITORIAL DIRECTION OF

Ralph W. Greenlaw* and Dwight E. Lee†

DECLINE AND FALL OF THE ROMAN EMPIRE—WHY DID IT COLLAPSE?†

THE PIRENNE THESIS—ANALYSIS, CRITICISM, AND REVISION*

THE CORONATION OF CHARLEMAGNE—WHAT DID IT SIGNIFY?*

THE RENAISSANCE—MEDIEVAL OR MODERN?*

MACHIAVELLI—CYNIC, PATRIOT, OR POLITICAL SCIENTIST?*

THE REFORMATION—MATERIAL OR SPIRITUAL?*

PROTESTANTISM AND CAPITALISM—THE WEBER THESIS AND ITS CRITICS*

THE ORIGINS OF THE ENGLISH CIVIL WAR—CONSPIRACY, CRUSADE, OR CLASS
    CONFLICT?*

THE REVOLUTION OF 1688—WHIG TRIUMPH OR PALACE REVOLUTION?†

THE GREATNESS OF LOUIS XIV—MYTH OR REALITY?*

THE EIGHTEENTH CENTURY REVOLUTION—FRENCH OR WESTERN?†

THE ECONOMIC ORIGINS OF THE FRENCH REVOLUTION—POVERTY OR PROSPERITY?*

METTERNICH, THE "COACHMAN OF EUROPE"—STATESMAN OR EVIL GENIUS?*

THE INDUSTRIAL REVOLUTION IN BRITAIN—TRIUMPH OR DISASTER?*

1848—A TURNING POINT?*

OTTO VON BISMARCK—A HISTORICAL ASSESSMENT*

THE "NEW IMPERIALISM"—ANALYSIS OF LATE NINETEENTH-CENTURY EXPANSION*

THE OUTBREAK OF THE FIRST WORLD WAR—WHO WAS RESPONSIBLE?*

THE RUSSIAN REVOLUTION AND BOLSHEVIK VICTORY—WHY AND HOW?*

THE VERSAILLES SETTLEMENT—WAS IT FOREDOOMED TO FAILURE?*

THE ETHIOPIAN CRISIS—TOUCHSTONE OF APPEASEMENT?*

THE NAZI REVOLUTION—GERMANY'S GUILT OR GERMANY'S FATE?*

THE BRITISH IN INDIA—IMPERIALISM OR TRUSTEESHIP?†

THE OUTBREAK OF THE SECOND WORLD WAR—DESIGN OR BLUNDER?†

Other volumes in preparation

PROBLEMS IN EUROPEAN CIVILIZATION

MACHIAVELLI

Cynic, Patriot, or Political Scientist?

EDITED WITH AN INTRODUCTION BY

De Lamar Jensen

BRIGHAM YOUNG UNIVERSITY

D. C. HEATH AND COMPANY · BOSTON

Library of Congress Catalog Card number 60-11574

Copyright © 1960 by D. C. Heath and Company

PRINTED IN THE UNITED STATES OF AMERICA

Table of Contents

POLITICAL SCIENTIST OR OPPORTUNIST?

THE CONTEMPORARY OUTLOOK

Introduction

I N more than four hundred years of evaluation and reinterpretation, few names
in European history have caused more disagreement and controversy than Machiavelli's. Nearly everyone who has written
on modern European history, and particularly on the Renaissance, agrees that Machiavelli was one of the most important
figures of the century, but rarely will they
concur on the reason for his prominence.
Why has this polemic continued so long
without sign of abating or losing its vigor?
Undoubtedly there can be many answers,
and among them certainly is the fact that
Machiavelli's written words deal with subjects of lasting and vital interest to all ages.
People of every generation must ask themselves the questions which Machiavelli
aroused. What is the relationship between
politics and morals? Does the end really
justify the means? What is the nature and
role of the state? How are liberty and
order to be balanced and maintained? To
the historian an infinite number of additional problems are suggested by the life
and writings of this Renaissance Florentine, from the question of his relationship
to the humanist writers of his time to the
methods and motives of his public and private life. For Machiavelli was not restricted
to one career, and each of them — diplomat,
secretary, statesman, military strategist, political philosopher, historian, man of letters
— offers a rich and rewarding field for scholarly investigation.

Much of the enigma connected with
Machiavelli results from the political confusion in Italy in his day and the role he
played in Italian public affairs. Born in
Florence in 1469, the son of a lawyer-
bureaucrat who provided him with a fairly
adequate education in religion, the classics,
and politics, Niccolò Machiavelli soon manifested both a desire and talent for governmental work. In 1494 he witnessed the
close of an epoch for Italy as French troops
under Charles VIII invaded from the north
and launched a half century of turmoil and
war throughout the peninsula. Florence
hesitated, then denounced the shaky government of Piero de' Medici and hailed the
French king as the deliverer prophesied by
Savonarola. A new republican government
was organized, and for the next four years
Florence was dominated by the austere
figure of the Dominican friar, until he met
his death in 1498. Then Machiavelli, at
the age of twenty-nine, was recognized by
the Signory for his administrative talents
and was elected to the responsible post of
Chancellor of the Second Chancery,[1]
where he also functioned in the Council of
the Ten of Liberty and Peace (formerly
Ten of War), the Florentine foreign office.
During the next fourteen years Machiavelli
served the republic faithfully, not only carrying out his secretarial and administrative
duties, but also serving as an able diplomat
and as personal advisor to Pietro Soderini,
Gonfalonier of Florence from 1502 to 1512.
As a functionary of the republic Machiavelli saw and participated in many of the
critical events at the turn of the century.
His diplomatic missions to the king of
France, to the countess of Imola and Forlì,
to the Emperor Maximilian, and to Cesare
Borgia, nefarious son of Pope Alexander
VI, taught him much about entangled
Italian politics and about the people who
manipulated affairs. Many of his official
letters and reports still exist and provide a

[1] See Nicolai Rubinstein, "The Beginning of
Niccolò Machiavelli's Career in the Florentine
Chancery," *Italian Studies*, XI (1956), 72–91,
for the most recent and helpful clarifications on
this misunderstood period of Machiavelli's life.

valuable source of insight into his political views.

With its continued French alliance and refusal to join the Holy League, Machiavelli knew that the Florentine position was not secure, and he persuaded the government to effect the military reorganization which he had long advocated — the replacement of mercenary troops with a trained and equipped citizens' militia. In 1508–09 Machiavelli's newly formed militia proved successful in the siege of Pisa, but when they faced veteran Spanish, German, and Italian troops in 1512 (engaged by the League to expel the French from Italy) they fled in confusion. In August of that year the Florentine republic fell and the Medici rule was restored. Machiavelli lost his post, was arrested for treason, and tortured on the rack, and finally went into exile at the ancestral home near San Casciano. At forty-three Machiavelli's public career had ended, but his much more celebrated life of letters was just beginning.

With little hope of regaining employment in the Medici government, Machiavelli returned to the cultivation of his writing talents, and within a few months he had produced a book which was to become the most notorious and shocking piece of literature of the Italian Renaissance, and which was to create a new and descriptive adjective in many languages. But before putting his pen to *The Prince,* Machiavelli apparently began a lengthy political commentary on the Roman history of Titus Livy.[2] These *Discourses* were never fully completed, but they still provide the closest thing we have to a systematic disclosure of Machiavelli's political thought. They reveal that he was basically a republican, with a rather keen conception of democratic values and limitations, who saw the state as a secu-

lar and autonomous structure relying for its survival upon human skills and mass support.

But Machiavelli was still too involved in the political upheavals of his own day to devote himself to such an academic task, and so he turned his full energies to the composition of *The Prince.* This little book of twenty-six very short chapters is the principal cause of Machiavelli's notoriety. In it he sets down a pattern of conduct and policy which a "wise" prince should follow if he desires success in winning and maintaining a kingdom. They are not the suggestions found in the moral teaching of Christianity, and are hardly the things we would expect from the conscientious civil servant who had devoted fourteen years of his life to the Florentine republic. Phrases such as "It is necessary for a prince, who wishes to maintain himself, to learn how not to be good," "A prudent ruler ought not to keep faith when by so doing it would be against his interest," "It is necessary to be a great feigner and dissembler," and "Men forget the murder of their fathers sooner than the loss of their patrimony" are fairly clear as phrases, but their meaning and intention leave much room for interpretation. Did Machiavelli mean, for example, that this is the way all princes *ought* to act, or merely that this is the way they *did* act — at least in the Italy of his day? Was he describing the true amoral and autonomous nature of politics and the state, or blasting the foundations of an effeminate and decadent Christian morality? Were his maxims to be taken as universally applicable truths of political science and statecraft, or as the pleas and recommendations of a patriotic Italian to a Medici prince to expel the foreigner and establish an independent Italian kingdom? Or was the whole book really a political satire written to ridicule the Medici tyranny? The elusive answers to these questions are still being sought.

Machiavelli's writing, following his retirement from public life, was not confined entirely to political commentary. He soon became quite active in literary circles, par-

[2] There is still a considerable amount of disagreement over the time sequence in the composition of *The Prince* and *The Discourses.* Here I have followed the more familiar order, advocated since 1927 by Federico Chabod and others. For the opposing views of Meinecke, Gilbert, Baron, and Hexter see the "Suggestions for Additional Reading" at the end of this book.

ticularly among the group which met frequently at the Oricellari Gardens. By 1520 he had written numerous short discourses, letters, and treatises, including a romanticized Life of *Castruccio Castracane* (the notorious fourteenth-century tyrant of Lucca) and *The Art of War*. The latter is considered by many Machiavelli scholars to be one of his three most important works. Yet during his own lifetime Machiavelli's notoriety came almost exclusively from his dramatic writings, particularly from his satirical comedy, *Mandragola*. The play itself has a rather fatuous plot, but the clever handling of the characters, and through them a humorous exposing of the foibles and baseness of Italian society of his day, make this one of the masterpieces of Renaissance comedy. It also established Machiavelli's fame as a talented dramatist. He wrote other plays: *Clizia, Prose Comedy, Comedy in Verse* (whose authorship is disputed), and *Andria;* but all of them are inferior to *Mandragola*. Numerous other minor works of both prose and poetry were written by him, including *The Marriage of the Arch-devil Belphagor,* a delightful prose comedy; the *Capitoli,* best of his short poems; *The Golden Ass,* an unfinished political satire in Dante-like verse; and *Dialogues* on sundry topics. Yet in many respects the most remarkable of Machiavelli's literary works was his *History of Florence,* commissioned by the Cardinal de' Medici in 1520, and still unfinished when Machiavelli died in 1527. Being less interested in "recreating" actual events and interpreting them in light of their environment than he was in using ready-made "lessons" from the past to illustrate and support his political views, Machiavelli's *History of Florence* emerges as a much more reliable guide to his political thought (for which it is seldom used) than to the real history of Florence.

Not many people, however, ever read Machiavelli's histories, and his reputation germinated almost entirely from the little booklet he wrote in a few months in 1513. *The Prince* was never published during its author's lifetime, and although it circulated quite widely in manuscript form, it seems to have caused little if any controversy. In 1532, five years after Machiavelli's death, it was published in Rome, and soon it was the subject of widespread political invective and moral reprobation. One of the earliest denunciations came from the pen of Cardinal Reginald Pole, who, in his *Apologia ad Carolum V. Caesarem* (1536), assailed *The Prince* as a product of the devil, and warned against its use by unscrupulous rulers (Henry VIII, for example) to undermine the *Respublica Christiana.* Pole's attack was echoed by other zealous clerics like Ambrosius Politi, bishop of Cosenza, and especially by the Portuguese Bishop Jeronimo Osorio. In 1559 all of Machiavelli's works were condemned by the Roman church and placed on the Index.

But Catholics held no monopoly on the condemnation of Machiavelli; Protestants too were shocked and alarmed by his open political immorality and cynicism. At the vanguard of their assault were the energetic French Huguenots who denounced Machiavelli in many of their polemical writings, including the famous *Vindiciae contra Tyrannos.* Of the numerous sixteenth-century books devoted to disparaging the works of Machiavelli, none was more popular, nor more influenced by the religious wars, than Innocent Gentillet's *Contre-Machiavel,* two chapters of which appear here as our first selection. Gentillet was a very literate Huguenot writer who drew on a humanistic legal background, and also a medieval-religious fear of strong monarchy, to refute the maxims of Machiavelli. Among other things, he contrasts the validity of the despotic political assertions in *The Prince* with the righteous examples of French administrative justice and efficiency, that is, down to the death of Henry II in 1559. The disruption and ferocity of the civil wars, which were tearing France apart when Gentillet published his book in 1576, were attributed by him to the infiltration of Machiavelli's ideas into France under the corrupt influence of the Italian queen mother, Catherine de' Medici. It is interesting to note also that Gentillet dedicated his book to the duke of Alençon (brother of the king and heir to the throne), who had convinced many of the Huguenots that he was their foremost friend and advocate.

In the seventeenth century the Spanish Jesuits took the lead in denouncing the Florentine writer, with the heaviest barrages coming from Pedro de Rivadeneira's *Tratado de la religión* (1595), and Claudio Clemente's *El machiavelismo degollado* ("Machiavellism Decapitated") (1637). These writers were particularly fearful of Machiavelli because of his shameless abasement of religion and his glorification of the state. But even the political writers of the period denounced Machiavelli's methods while modestly agreeing with his motives of promoting the secular political state. By the eighteenth century Machiavelli had become a byword in every language and among every social class. Clerics, philosophers, historians, and statesmen all inveighed against him with equal vigor. Even monarchs, whether they followed his dictums or not (and most of them did), occasionally took the opportunity to speak or write against him. The classic example of an attack by a political despot against the political despotism of Machiavelli is the *Antimachiavel* of Frederick the Great, from which an excerpt is used here as our second selection. Frederick wrote his treatise before he became king of Prussia, but he saw such hazardous implications in *The Prince,* which might cause his subjects to suspect and distrust him, that he felt obligated to try to nullify this effect. At least there was no harm in letting his people think he frowned upon the principles of Machiavellism. It has been observed that Machiavelli would have commended him for the move — what could be more astute or more in tune with *The Prince* than a denunciation of it! But whatever the motive, *L'Antimachiavel* was popular from the moment of its publication. Nor was Frederick alone in his condemnation of Machiavelli. The very nature of the Enlightenment, with its great stress on Natural Law and morals, made it extremely difficult for the *philosophes* to comprehend Machiavelli's apparent pragmatism.

In very sharp contrast to the attacks of Gentillet and Frederick II is the defense of Machiavelli offered by Max Lerner in our third selection. Lerner supports Machiavelli's views, not because they are good or praiseworthy, but because they are statements of fact. He sees the maxims as outstanding examples of political realism, undeceived by the wishes and idealism of what "ought" to be, and keenly aware of what "is." He pictures Machiavelli as an enlightened and liberal republican whose ideas, especially according to *The Discourses,* are aimed toward the achievement of high political goals through the recognition and acceptance of realities. This changed attitude of the twentieth century toward Machiavelli is likewise reflected in the next selection, by Benedetto Croce, who, writing in the mid-1920's, proposed what has become a fundamental treatise on Machiavelli. Croce disagrees that Machiavelli's politics are immoral, since the very nature of politics as a separate and autonomous entity precludes the use of that term in connection with it. Politics has an existence and morality independent of private and social life, and this autonomy is vital to the proper functioning of the state. Machiavelli's divorce of politics from all other considerations, including morality, therefore, seemed to Croce to be the fundamental feature of Machiavelli's thought.

But it required a long period of reinterpretation and adjustment before views such as those of Lerner and Croce superseded the hostile charges of men like Gentillet and Frederick II. Although opinion was overwhelmingly anti-Machiavellian during the first two and one half centuries after the publication of *The Prince,* there were a few writers who ventured to suggest a more favorable interpretation of him, but their views were generally considered to be immature or even treasonous. Justus Lipsius, sixteenth-century Flemish humanist and stoic, was one of the first to speak favorably of Machiavelli's political writings, although he too thought *The Prince* was unnecessarily unscrupulous. His contemporary, the Italian-English jurist, Alberico Gentili, took a bolder stand in favor of Machiavelli, on the ground that *The Prince* was actually intended to be a burlesque of despotism and tyranny rather than a guide for its promotion. This idea of *The Prince* as a satire gained several prominent adherents in the next two centuries, among them Spinoza, Rousseau, and Vittorio Alfieri. The latter's *Del principe e delle lettere* (1796) lauds the "divine genius of our Machiavelli" and refers to him as the only real philosopher Italy could claim.

Along with the social, economic, and political revolutions which ushered in the nineteenth century, came a revolution in European ideas and values which greatly affected historical writing and interpretation. Of the many new "isms" which occupied European thought, one of the most fundamental and influential was nationalism. As people began to think and write more about nationalism, it became inevitable that some would soon re-evaluate Machiavelli in the light of this new outlook. In his *Briefe zur Beförderung der Humanität,* published in 1797, Herder suggested that Machiavelli's motivation was a desire for the national independence of Italy, and during Prussia's death struggle with Napoleon, both Hegel and Fichte gave expression to this same idea, calling upon their countrymen to take heed of Machiavelli's advice. Leopold von Ranke took a similar stand as early as 1824 in one of his earliest pieces of historical writing.

As might be imagined, this interpretation took deep roots in Italy, and as the unification of that country was gradually achieved, more Italian scholars came to see the correlation between their own time and Machiavelli's. Pasquale Villari saw Machiavelli in this light as he wrote his classic *Life and Times of Niccolò Machiavelli.* Our fifth selection is taken from the conclusion to volume II of this standard biography. Villari justifies Machiavelli's unethical means for achieving unification on the grounds that they were the methods of his day and the only ones offering any hope for success. In his monumental work, *La vita e gli scritti di Niccolò Machiavelli,* Villari's contemporary, Oreste Tommasini, also pictured Machiavelli as a dedicated Italian nationalist. Likewise the outstanding Italian literary critic of the nineteenth century, Francesco De Sanctis, lauded Machiavelli's unvarying service to his country and to mankind. Like Villari, De Sanctis witnessed the final unification of Italy, and praised Machiavelli as one of its noblest patriots, who was devoted to country, reason, intelligence, and to manliness. An excerpt from De Sanctis appears as selection six.

This popular view of Machiavelli was not restricted to Italian writers, nor even to the nineteenth century. The next article, by Sir Richard Lodge, illustrates an equally unqualified acceptance of Machiavelli's nationalism. Lodge defends the thesis that Machiavelli wrote "to a particular prince in peculiar and special circumstances and for his guidance to a definite objective"; the objective being the liberation of Italy from the foreigner. In this burst of patriotism Machiavelli fancied himself to be the sixteenth-century Cavour who would spark the Italian unification. The last article in this section is by Felix Gilbert, who discloses another dimension to the problem. Gilbert carefully analyzes the concept of nationalism in Machiavelli, and in his contemporaries, and shows how mistaken Villari, De Sanctis, and Lodge are in assuming that it meant the same thing to Machiavelli as it did to the nationalist patriots of the nineteenth century. Gilbert's article has opened many completely new vistas into this thoroughly intriguing subject.

Ranke and his esteemed British contemporary, Lord Macaulay, both spoke out for a better understanding of the life and conditions in Renaissance Italy before judging Machiavelli too harshly. Macaulay's famous "Essay on Machiavelli," published in the *Edinburgh Review* of March, 1827, was not as complete a vindication of the Florentine as were the writings of De Sanctis and others later in the century, but it did affirm that Machiavelli's depravity and iniquity were merely symptomatic of the evils and vices of his day. This view, that Machiavelli's thought and writings were the direct reflection of his environment and that he therefore wrote primarily as a "mirror of the times," gained considerable strength in the late nineteenth and early twentieth centuries. This interpretation emphasizes the restrictive nature of Machiavelli's statements, insisting that they applied only to a particular time and situation and were not to be construed as universally applicable principles or laws. The selection by L. A. Burd, published in 1891, is a good example of this thinking. Burd insists that Machiavelli was speaking only for his own time and locality, and that taken out of this context he becomes distorted and meaningless. Lord Acton's overly celebrated introduction to Burd's edition of *Il Principe* concurred that Machiavelli "was simply a faithful observer of facts who described the fell necessity that governs narrow territories and unstable fortunes," but he also believed that most of the forces extant in the world of Machiavelli still prevailed in his own, and therefore Machiavelli became an observer of the present world as well.

Federico Chabod's subtle and penetrating studies of Machiavelli are perhaps the best illustration yet of the view under consideration, a view which many contemporary historians prefer to call the Italian tradition, but which could be defined with equal validity as the historical approach. Chabod sees the development of Machiavelli's thought as a reflection of, and a response to, the actual political and social conditions and events of his time. In the excerpt used here, Chabod turns away from the nationalist interpretation, and instead places great emphasis on Machiavelli's concrete political and military judgments which are contained in his political writings, particularly in *The Art of War*. In so doing he illustrates the cause-and-effect relationship between Machiavelli's environment and his writings. Herbert Butterfield (selection number 11) also shows that Machiavelli was a man of his times, but he emphasizes the fact that Machiavelli felt nothing but contempt for his own contemporaries, preferring always to show his greater affection and admiration for the ancient Romans. Butterfield believes that Machiavelli's historical method was basic to his entire political outlook and that he discloses this in his *Discourses* and *Prince* as much as in his histories. On the restrictive nature of Machiavelli's intentions, Butterfield goes even further than Burd, observing that Machiavelli not only restricted his analysis to a certain time and place, but to a certain abnormal group — the political tyrants. Yet in spite of this it is obvious from the flavor of Butterfield's writing that he stands at the opposite pole from Burd and Chabod in his basic dislike of Machiavelli.

The next two selections illustrate an interpretation which has developed out of the peculiar environmental pattern of the late nineteenth and early twentieth centuries, but which did not take articulate form until in the twentieth: Machiavelli as a scientist — as a true analyst of political situations and events, and formulator of general patterns and laws of political behavior. This view has gained wide popularity among political scientists and also among a substantial number of historians. According to Ernst Cassirer (selection number 12), Machiavelli approached the formulation of political theory "in the same way in which a physician describes the symptoms of a certain illness," warning against L. A. Burd's thesis, which he calls a "political illusion" and "the historian's fallacy." Yet he takes his place along with most modern historians in his recognition of the sharp contradiction that exists between Machiavelli's written doctrines and his personal life and character. In the next selection, Leonardo Olschki supports Cassirer's interpretation, and adds another dimension to it with his analysis of Machiavelli's scientific methods, showing that to a far greater extent than any of his contemporaries (even those popularly associated with the beginnings of science, like Da Vinci and Galileo) Machiavelli possessed a detached, impartial, scientific mind. Just as Galileo, by his attitudes and method, laid the foundations of natural science, so Machiavelli, by a similar approach to man and his institutions, founded the science of politics. How different from the immoral cynic of the sixteenth, seventeenth, and eighteenth centuries, or from the "involved" nationalist patriot of the nineteenth! The triumph of science in the twentieth century was also a triumph for Machiavelli. But Joseph Kraft takes strong issue with these views, and, in the article which follows, makes a very revealing exposé of Machiavelli's "objectivity," showing that his "scientific" and "detached" methods were as unscientific and prejudiced as those of most of his contemporaries. Kraft concludes that if Machiavelli must continue to be considered a political scientist it is a very sad commentary on the current state of political science.

The decade following World War I saw the publication of some of the most thoughtful and influential studies on Machiavelli. With the issues of "war guilt," "international morality," "reparations," and "self-determination" adding new dimensions to political thought, the relationship of Machiavellism to statecraft and to the concept of the state was again re-examined. Friedrich Meinecke's profound study of the concept of *raison d'état* in Machiavelli and in other political thinkers, published in 1924, considers Machiavelli as the cornerstone of the modern concept of the state, and of the emergence of *Realpolitik*. He contends further that the very essence of the development of the modern state is "the struggle for and against Machiavellism." Part of his analysis is reproduced here as selection number fifteen. Francesco Ercole carried this concept even further in the

next few years as he saw and accepted the fulfillment of Machiavelli's statecraft in the Fascist state of Mussolini.

With the specter of totalitarianism haunting the world in the late 1930's and early 1940's, many scholars saw in the Nazi and Fascist dictatorships the inevitable maturation of Machiavellism. Many of them took up their pens to combat the leviathan. These twentieth-century denunciations of Machiavelli, however, took a much more analytical and subtle form than did those of the sixteenth to eighteenth centuries, although they still emphasized the immorality and cynicism of Machiavelli. Whereas the earlier opponents always equated political and private morality, the modern critics recognize the separation and contend that in the long run political morality, both domestic and international, must be raised to a higher plane than Machiavelli had relegated it if society is to progress, or even continue to exist. The next two selections, by G. P. Gooch and Jacques Maritain, develop this view. Gooch emphasizes the moral foundations of political society as revealed by the leading political thinkers of England, and proclaims that Machiavelli erred seriously in his basic evaluation of mankind. "The will to power," Gooch says, "is not the sole key to human nature," and all of the higher impulses which also motivate men are ignored or denied by Machiavelli, whose political philosophy stems from an unrealistically narrow base. Machiavelli's "realism" then is as much a myth to Gooch as his "scientific method" is to Kraft. Maritain challenges Machiavelli's assertion that the goal of politics is the supremacy of the state, and proposes that its ultimate aim is rather the common good of individual man, and therefore it cannot be separated from ethics. Politics cannot be autonomous! From this foundation he demonstrates the illegitimacy of Machiavellism and speaks out for a reassertion of moral courage and political justice — the only effective weapons against this "knighthood of human degradation."

At the present time Machiavelli studies

continue to appear in ever-increasing numbers, and there is no sign of any diminution in the near future. Not only is the interest continuing to mount, but current views seem to indicate as great a disagreement in interpretation as ever before. Two trends at least are very apparent in contemporary scholarship: One of these is the great quantity and high quality of recent Italian literature on the subject, and the other is the noticeable increase of interest in Machiavelli in the United States, perhaps reflecting the new post-war role of this country in world political affairs. Typical of the excellence of contemporary Italian scholarship are the penetrating studies of the life and thought of Machiavelli by Federico Chabod, Roberto Ridolfi, Luigi Russo, and most recently by Gennaro Sasso. At universities and colleges throughout the United States, scholars are likewise analyzing, comparing, and re-evaluating Machiavelli. Felix Gilbert's numerous monographs on many phases of Machiavelli's life and thought, Hans Baron's studies of the composition of his political writings, J. H. Hexter's analyses of the semantics of *The Prince,* and Leo Strauss's critical reflections on Machiavelli's teachings are examples of the variety and vigor of this trend.

Our final selection, a stimulating new look at Machiavelli by Garrett Mattingly, reaffirms our observation that serious and original contributions are still being made to Machiavelli studies. Mattingly's provocative suggestion is that *The Prince* be viewed as a political satire, written for the purpose of exposing and ridiculing despotism, rather than as a cynical manual for encouraging it or a detached and scientific analysis of it. This is a view which has not been seriously held since the late eighteenth century, but the compelling logic of Mattingly's argument, as well as the insight and precision with which he develops his evidence, makes this an interpretation which cannot be neglected in the future, even by those who will disagree with it. This pungent article proves again that there is still ample room for painstaking scholarship and discerning re-evaluation in this important field. Many new questions must still be formulated and posed, old ones examined and reaffirmed or rejected, and new information and viewpoints considered before we are ready to close the case with a final answer to the query, "Was Machiavelli a Machiavellian?"

[In order to conserve space, all of the footnotes appearing in the original articles have been omitted, except for those which were considered essential to the clarification and accuracy of the author's text.]

The Conflict of Opinion

"I venture now to take up the defence of humanity against this monster who wants to destroy it; with reason and justice I dare to oppose sophistry and crime; and I put forth these reflections on *The Prince* of Machiavelli, chapter by chapter, so that the antidote may be found immediately following the poison."

— Frederick II

"May I venture a guess as to the reason why we still shudder slightly at Machiavelli's name? It is not only the tradition I have described. It is our recognition that the realities he described *are* realities; that men, whether in politics, in business or in private life, do *not* act according to their professions of virtue."

— Max Lerner

"When, on completing his analysis . . . Machiavelli proceeds to draw his conclusions, then at last the practical side and real aim of his work are clearly seen. It is a question of achieving the unity of his Italian motherland and of delivering it from foreign rule. . . . This is an enterprise only to be undertaken by a Prince-reformer, and by the means suggested and imposed by history and experience."

— Pasquale Villari

"This is true Machiavellism, alive, indeed even young. It is the program of the modern world, developed, corrected, amplified, and more or less realized. . . . Let us therefore be proud of our Machiavelli. Glory to him whenever a part of the ancient edifice crumbles! And glory to him when some new part is added!"

— Francesco De Sanctis

"*The Prince* was never meant except for Italians, and Italians too of a given period; indeed, we may go further, and ask whether it was ever intended even for all Italians; it certainly bears the stamp of what a modern writer might call an esoteric treatise."

— L. A. Burd

"*The Prince* is neither a moral nor an immoral book; it is simply a technical book. In a technical book we do not seek rules of ethical conduct, of good and evil. . . . Machiavelli studied political actions in the same way as a chemist studies chemical reactions. Assuredly a chemist who prepares in his laboratory a strong poison is not responsible for its effects. . . . Machiavelli's *Prince* contains many dangerous and poisonous things, but he looks at them with the coolness and indifference of a scientist. He gives his political prescriptions."

— Ernst Cassirer

"Not so clean and neat . . . is the contention that Machiavelli, a dispassionate observer of the facts, is the Darwin of politics. Rather this contention is messy with black marks. Machiavelli did not observe the facts closely. His deductions were, in many cases, illogical. He utterly misread the general military picture of the day. . . . The poor man appears to be as much a poet as a scientist."

— JOSEPH KRAFT

"Despite the number and eminence of his disciples, I believe that Machiavelli is unfair to mankind. The professed realist only saw a limited portion of the vast field of experience. The will to power is not the sole key to human nature. . . . If man were indeed the unruly and perfidious animal that he believes, *The Prince* might be accepted as a recipe for making the best of a bad job. But the broad testimony of modern history suggests that the average man rises above this level."

— G. P. GOOCH

"I suppose it is possible to imagine that a man who has seen his country enslaved, his life's work wrecked and his career with it, and has, for good measure, been tortured within an inch of his life should thereupon go home and write a book intended to teach his enemies the proper way to maintain themselves, writing all the time, remember, with the passionless objectivity of a scientist in a laboratory. It must be possible to imagine such behavior, because Machiavelli scholars do imagine it and accept it without a visible tremor. But it is a little difficult for the ordinary mind to compass."

— GARRETT MATTINGLY

IMMORAL CYNIC OR LIBERAL REALIST?

Is It Better to Be Loved or Feared?

INNOCENT GENTILLET

One of the most widely circulated attacks on Machiavelli in the sixteenth century was the *Contre-Machiavel* of Innocent Gentillet (1550–1595), active Huguenot lawyer and writer from Dauphiné and Geneva. Gentillet was well trained in law and functioned in the Parlement de Grenoble and as head of the Tribunal de Justice at Die. As an ardent Huguenot he was a vigorous pamphleteer for the cause of Calvinism in France, writing numerous tracts against the crown, the papacy, and the Catholic League. His famous critique of Machiavelli was originally written in Latin in 1571, then published anonymously in a French edition at Lausanne in 1576. The selection here, taken from the first French edition, examines the subject of cruelty and clemency among rulers as interpreted by Machiavelli in chapter XVII of *The Prince*.

THIS maxim, *oderint dum metuant*, meaning "let them hate that they might fear," is a saying or proverb attributed by the ancients to the Tyrants. As we have shown elsewhere, the same proverb, according to Suetonius, was usurped by Gaius Caligula and put into practice during his reign, with results similar to those of all princes who prefer being feared to being loved. The Emperor Tiberius chose to soften the proverb by favoring the exercise of fear but not of hate. For he used to say, as in another adage, *oderint dum probent*, "let them hate that they might obey." But it seems that he unwisely linked hatred with approbation, for he who hates does not consent willingly and he who approves does not at the same time hate. In short, all such dictums and proverbs are tyrants' schemes which the ancients always attributed to them and which furthermore they always practiced. Nero, for example, when he demonstrated that he was greatly feared and dreaded for his cruelties, boasted that not one of those who had preceded him as emperor had really understood how to command, nor had wielded the authority to make himself obeyed. But one must himself understand this power and feel certain that poorly exercised authority brings hatred upon him who exercises it, and hatred brings ruin and defeat. Just as with Caligula and with Tiberius so it is with all those who seek to make themselves feared through hate rather than through love.

As for Machiavelli's assertion that the prince is feared according to his will and pleasure, this would be very well for him if it were true, since thus he would always be feared to the extent that nobody would oppose his commands and desires and everyone would simply obey and submit to his yoke. But experience shows us the contrary, and we are forced to see and rec-

From Innocent Gentillet, *Discourse sur les moyens de bien gouverner et maintenir en bonne paix un Royaume ou autre Principauté. Contre Nicolas Machiavel Florentin.* (Lausanne, 1576), pp. 375–81. Translated by the editor.

1

ognize that the prince cannot maintain obedience if the commands he gives are disagreeable and found by the people to be unjust. Because on the very first opportunity which arises they will throw off the yoke and refuse to submit to oppression, except as force and compulsion are maintained. And inasmuch as no amount of force and compulsion can really be sustained over a long period of time — since nothing that by nature is violent is durable — it follows that distasteful orders are not observed long, and soon that allegiance which was based upon fear is straightway torn apart. For the equality and justice of a decree are its very nerves, and just as a body without nerves cannot move (unless it be thrown like a rock), so a command, which because of a lack of fairness is disagreeable to the people, will never be put into much action or practice; or if it is it will only receive a token obedience.

Now concerning Machiavelli's pronouncement that it is very difficult for a prince to be both feared and loved at the same time; this is entirely erroneous, for there is nothing easier for a prince than to obtain them both, as sound reason will attest. For inasmuch as it is certain that a prince who will keep the peace for his subjects and guard them from oppression, while at the same time prosecuting those who would try to tyrannize them, and who will protect their liberties by punishing violators of it, and keep order throughout the country so that commerce might move freely and safely without the imposition of new taxes and tributes, and who will be the minister of justice to each and every one, I say it is certain that such a prince will be greatly loved by his subjects. But what about fear? When it is understood that he will be a minister of justice for all, without support, favor, or corruption, not allowing misdemeanors to go unpunished, and not being too liberal in giving favors unless they are founded on reason and equality; it is unquestionable but that he will also be dreaded, not just throughout his own country but also in foreign lands.

As an example of this I might cite all of the good emperors of old, such as Augustus, Trajan, Hadrian, Antoninus, and others, who were dreaded, loved, and revered all at the same time. I could also cite almost all of our ancient kings of France who through justice were feared not only by their own subjects but likewise by all of their neighbors. It is apparent that this reputation of justice, which they had, was, as we read in the histories, the reason foreign princes submitted their differences to the judgment of the *Cour des Pairs* of France. And because they did carry out honest judgment do you think they were hated? Not even by the wicked, who, in spite of the contradiction of their own lives, were forced by their conscience to appreciate and admire justice and virtue. And since the kings of France did not have to love their subjects, being the good rulers that they were, it is obvious that the French people were this way naturally, not even knowing how to hate their king no matter how depraved he might be. Thus they attribute all the vices and mistakes to one or another of the governors and counselors rather than to the king. And in truth, if princes always recognized the good men near them they would never become rotted in vice (much less to the detriment of the public); so it would be a good thing, as we have said before, if the government of a country were entrusted more to the counselors of the prince than to the prince himself.

II

This maxim ["Love is held by a chain of obligation which, men being selfish, is broken whenever it serves their purpose; but fear is maintained by a dread of punishment which never fails." *The Prince*, Chap. XVII], just as the preceding one, is a truly tyrannical precept. For as the poet Aeschylus said:

In every Tyrant there is a common evil
To neither trust nor believe in any friend.

This is the reason Denis, Tyrant of Sicily, had a strong house built in which he might live securely, surrounded by deep trenches filled with water and across which no one could pass except over drawbridges. Each evening he raised the drawbridges himself and removed the pegs which were used to fasten the pieces of the bridge together, carried these pegs affectionately to bed with him, and the next morning returned them again to their places. He also made his children learn to be barbers so they could cut his hair and beard, because he trusted no one else in the world to do it. But the Emperor Commodus (who was a cruel tyrant) had even further hesitations, for he trusted absolutely no person to trim his hair and beard and so he singed himself with a candle.[1] I will let you decide whether such men are miserable or not, having a conscience which torments them to the extent that they judge the entire world to be their enemy until they dare not trust a soul, and they are thus in continual fear and torment.

Very different from this doctrine of Machiavelli is the exhortation given by the good King Micipsa of Numidia just prior to his death when he admonished Jugurtha and his other children to always maintain love and understanding for one another. "It is not (he said) by powerful forces, large armies, or great wealth, that a prince should hold and maintain his state, but rather by friends who attained their position neither by force of arms nor by gold or silver but by good services and loyalty. Now who ought to be a more loyal friend than a brother is to his brother? Or who can have faith in one who would be an enemy to his own blood? If you are upright I will leave you a kingdom which is strong and secure, but one weak and fragile if you are unworthy. For through cooperation small things become great, but through discord great ones are ruined." Here then is an exhortation, brief but very weighty, to show the value of having good friends and of maintaining friendship and loyalty within the family. This is similar

[1] Commodus eventually met his death by poison. [Editor's note]

to the remonstrance given by Sulla to King Bocchus of Mauritania. "We are very pleased," he said, "that you strive rather to be a friend than an enemy of the Roman people. For since the beginning of their rise the Roman people, being poor, have always preferred to win friends to acquiring slaves and serfs, and have deemed it safer to command free men than men under coercion. Now, King Bocchus, you cannot find a better friendship than ours; one that can support you and help you, and one that will not wish something in return. And in truth neither we nor others can have too many friends."

The friendship and the friends that a prince should have won by good and just government may serve him tolerably well in keeping an eye on everyone in the state, so that it will not be necessary to be on the alert for misfortunes when he travels in the realm. Just as the good Emperor Trajan used to do when he frequently chose to see and visit his friends, accompanied only by four or five gentlemen and without any military guard. And the same thing used to be done by our ancient kings of France, who knew nothing of arms and other military gear that is used today, as they ordinarily travelled with no more than a company of gentlemen carrying only their swords.

Friendship (said Cicero) is the true bond of all human society and whosoever wishes to do away with good will among men (as Machiavelli did among princes) will succeed in eliminating all pleasure, consolation, contentment, and security that exists among men. For a friend is another self, with whom we share in our prosperity, and as we share it we rejoice in its growth. Thus we console ourselves and each other in our adversity, and our pain and sorrow are reduced by half when we have someone upon whom we can, by friendly communication, unload the bitterness in our heart. Moreover, just as it is that we are always dazzled and blinded by our own acts, our friend notes our faults and gently reminds us of them, and he gives us counsel about our affairs which we would never be able to see by ourselves. In short, human life without friendship resembles nothing more than a woeful existence, destitute of the principal sweetness that one might otherwise garner from human society; just as Cicero, Plutarch, and other great philosophers have wisely spoken, and whose wish I echo, that the worth and utility of friendship might be fully understood.

I do not wish to deny that one does find many such friends as those spoken of by Machiavelli, who pretend to be our friends while they connive to reap a great profit from us, and who are very solicitous when they see that we are not in particular need, but who turn away from us completely in our distress. There are obviously only too many of such kind, and we are too often deceived. But it is far from the truth to disdain all of the good because of the bad, instead of criticizing the particular things that are worthless. For amid the good wheat grow the tares which on the outside resemble the grain itself; and among the finest grass grow noxious weeds which on sight appear to be beautiful and good. And yet we must not throw out good wheat in order to avoid the tares, nor good and beautiful herbs because of the noxious ones. Rather it is essential to try as much as possible to recognize and separate the bad from the good.

And on the manner to choose good friends, the observation of Augustus Caesar is worth noting, for he did not readily keep everyone in his friendship and intimacy without previously sounding out and proving their virtue, faithfulness, and loyalty. Those whom he recognized as being virtuous men and who told him frankly the truth of all things (as did his good and wise Macaenas), and who did not flatter him, and who busied themselves earnestly and with good will in the assignments he gave them after they were well tried, these he took to him as his friends. Since it was such a long and difficult process to thus gain people into familiar amity, and since once they were won he never again forsook them, they continued constantly in his friendship. Even adversity is likewise a true touchstone of friendship to test which are the real and which are the sham friends; for when a man falls into some labyrinth at the crossroads his pretended friends go on, while the true ones tarry with him. This is what the poet Euripides said:

Prosperity brings friends both good and poor;
Adversity but the good, who fail nevermore.

Should a Prince Keep Faith?

FREDERICK THE GREAT

The notorious literary assault against Machiavelli by Frederick II, on the eve of his accession to the throne of Prussia, is even more vigorous than Gentillet's. Frederick wrote his treatise, entitled *Réfutation du Prince de Machiavel*, in 1739, then submitted it to Voltaire for his reading and revision. Voltaire altered the form somewhat, changed the title to the familiar *L'Antimachiavel*, and had it published at The Hague in 1740. In addition to his applause of Frederick's defense of "virtue, honesty, and true religion against the degrading effects of Machiavellism," Voltaire, in a later edition, praised the Prussian king's "noble, energetic, and for the most part pure" French prose, which he suggested "can greatly polish our language as well as reform our morals." The first part of our selection is Frederick's introduction to his essay, and the second is his commentary on the scandalous eighteenth chapter of *The Prince*.

MACHIAVELLI'S *The Prince* is to matters of morality what Spinoza's works are to matters of faith. Spinoza sapped the foundations of faith, stopping at nothing short of overturning the entire edifice of religion; while Machiavelli corrupted politics, and in so doing hoped to destroy the very precepts of sound morality. The errors of the one are only errors of speculation, while those of the other are errors of practice. Nevertheless, it is seen that the theologians have sounded the tocsin and raised the call to arms against Spinoza, so that the form of his works has been refuted, while Divinity has been defended against his attacks; yet Machiavelli has only been harassed by a few moralists, and in spite of them and in spite of his pernicious morality, he has maintained his preeminence in the chair of politics down to the present.

I venture now to take up the defense of humanity against this monster who wants to destroy it; with reason and justice I dare to oppose sophistry and crime; and I put forth these reflections on *The Prince* of Machiavelli, chapter by chapter, so that the antidote may be found immediately following the poison.

I have always regarded *The Prince* of Machiavelli as one of the most dangerous works that have ever been poured out on the world. It is a book which must fall naturally into the hands of the princes, and into those of others who have an interest in politics. Nor is it unlikely that ambitious young men, whose heart and judgment have not yet matured enough to enable them to distinguish between good and evil, will be corrupted by these maxims that flatter their passions.

But if it is bad to seduce the innocence of men whose influence is only lightly felt in the affairs of the world, it is that much worse to pervert the princes who must govern the people, administer justice, and set an example for their subjects, and to be, by their bounty, magnanimity, and mercy, the living images of the Divine.

Floods which ravage the countries, lightning which reduces villages to ashes, and plague and pestilence which desolate the

From *Oeuvres de Frédéric II, Roi de Prusse.* (Berlin: Chez Voss et Fils, Decker et Fils, et chez Treuttel, 1789), Vol. II, pp. 5–11, 86–94. Translated by the editor.

provinces, are not as disastrous and fatal to the world as the perilous morals and the unloosed passions of kings. These scourges of nature last only for a time; they ravage only some countries; and the losses, however painful, can still be repaired. But the crimes of kings leave the people of whole nations to suffer for years.

In this manner the rulers have the power within them to do great good or harm according to their will. How deplorable a situation a people are in when they have so much to fear from the abuse of the power of their sovereign, when their property is a prey to the avarice of their prince, their liberty to his caprice, their peace to his ambition, their safety to his perfidy, and their lives to his cruelty. This then is the tragic picture of a state ruled by a prince of Machiavelli's creation.

I cannot finish this preface without saying a word to the people who believe that Machiavelli wrote about the things that princes actually do rather than what they ought to do; a belief which has pleased many in the world because it has a flavor of satire.

Those who have pronounced this decisive judgment against the rulers have, undoubtedly, been seduced by the examples of some corrupt princes, contemporaries of Machiavelli and cited by him, and by the lives of other tyrants who have been a disgrace to humanity. I plead with these censors to remember that since the ruler is most strongly subjected to seduction it is necessary that he have more than ordinary virtue in order to resist, and that it should not, therefore, be a surprising thing, among a group as large as that of the princes, to find some bad ones among the good. Among the Roman emperors, where we can count Nero, Caligula, and Tiberius, the world can rejoice in being able to also remember the virtuous names of Titus, Trajan, and Antoninus. It is an injustice therefore to condemn an entire group because of the actions of a few of its members.

Only the names of the good princes ought to be recorded in history and those of the rest allowed to die along with their indolence, injustice, and their crimes. The number of history books would thus be diminished a great deal, but humanity would profit from it, and the honor of living in the true record of history, to see one's name pass through the future centuries into eternity would be the compensation for a life of virtue. The book of Machiavelli would then no longer infect the schools of politics, his numerous contradictions would be scorned, and the world would be convinced that the true politics of kings, based only on justice, wisdom, and goodness, is preferable in every sense to the disconnected and horrible system which Machiavelli has had the impudence to present to the public.

* * *

This preceptor of tyrants dares to assert here that princes ought to abuse the world with their dissimulation; to this I must take issue and oppose him.

It is well known that the public is sometimes curious; an animal that sees everything, hears everything, and repeats everything it has seen and heard. If this public curiosity looks into the conduct of private persons it is for the purpose of adding amusement to idle hours, but when it aspires to judge the character of princes it is for personal use. Princes are also more exposed than any other men to the rationalizations and judgments of the world, for they are like the stars which the astronomers scrutinize with their telescopes and astrolabes, as the courtiers follow them daily and report their observations. The slightest gesture or glance is looked upon as a betrayal and the people will form judgments from their conjectures. In a word, it is as difficult for great princes to conceal their vices and their true character from so many observers as it is for the sun to hide its spots.

Even though the mask of dissimulation may cover the natural deformities of a prince for a time, he cannot wear it forever without lifting it at times, if only to breathe, and just once is sufficient to satisfy the curious. Artifice and dissimulation then will be of no further use to that prince; the cunning discrepancy between his words and his deeds will then be useless. Men are not judged by their speech alone — this would always be a mistake — but by their actions and their words. Against such repeated examination falsehood and hypocrisy cannot endure. No one can afford to be other than himself. He must ultimately be the character he wants the world to think he is; otherwise it is not the public that he is deceiving, but himself. Sixtus V, Philip II, and Cromwell are known to the world as hypocrites and as enterprisers, but not as virtuous men. No prince who follows the maxims of Machiavelli, no matter how able he is, can exhibit the character of virtue which he does not possess in place of the crimes which are his own.

Machiavelli reasons no better on the motives which should impel princes toward knavery and hypocrisy. The ingenious and perverted application which he gives to the fable of the centaur is inconclusive, because, although the centaur was half man and half horse, does it follow that princes should be cunning and savage? He must be proud to be able to dogmatize crime and to employ such fabulous arguments, in order to uphold his doctrines. But here is the most erroneous reasoning we have ever seen: statecraft requires that a prince have the qualities of both the lion and the fox — the lion so he can overthrow the wolves, the fox so he can be crafty — and Machiavelli concludes, "Therefore, it is not necessary for a prince to keep his word." Here you see a conclusion without premises. Is not the good doctor of crime ashamed to pour out the lessons of impiety?

If one is to ascribe any probity or good sense to the entangled thoughts of Machiavelli it can perhaps be done only in the following manner. The world is like a game of cards in which some of the players are honest but others are cheaters. Therefore, a prince who wants to play in such a game, if he does not wish to be taken, ought to be well acquainted with all of the tricks of the game, not in order to practice them

himself, but to avoid becoming a dupe of the others.

Let us return to the downfall of our statesman. "Since all men," he said, "are villainous and will not keep their word with you, there is no obligation for you to keep faith with them." But first of all, notice the contradiction; for the author says a moment later that the dissembler will always find men simple enough for him to deceive. But how can this be reconciled? For if all men are knaves and scoundrels how can you find enough fools to be deceived?

It is, in fact, completely false that the world is composed only of villains. It would be very misanthropic indeed not to see that in every society there are many honest men, and that the greatest majority are neither good nor bad. But if Machiavelli had not supposed the world to be made of scoundrels what would he have based his abominable maxim on? Even if we were to suppose that men are really as bad as Machiavelli sees them, this does not mean that we ought to imitate them. If Cartouche plundered, pillaged, and killed, I would conclude that he was a miserable wretch who ought to be punished rather than that I ought to pattern my conduct after his. If there is no longer any honor and virtue in the world, said Charles the Wise, it should be the princes who will recover its traces.

After the author has proved the necessity of crime he then encourages his disciples by the ease with which it can be committed. "Those who understand the art of dissimulation," he says, "will always find men simple enough to be their dupes." Or in other words: your neighbor is a fool and you are an intelligent person; therefore, it follows that you ought to deceive him since he is a fool. These are syllogisms, however, for which students of Machiavelli have been hanged and broken on the rack.

But this politician is not content with having demonstrated, according to his method of reasoning, the satisfaction of crime; he proceeds to reveal the advantages of perfidy. But troublesome to him is the fact that Cesare Borgia, the greatest of all villains, the most perfidious of men, who was the hero of Machiavelli, was in the end completely wretched. Machiavelli guards against speaking of him on this occasion since he was not a good example of the validity of his point. But where else would you expect to find such examples if not on the register of criminals or in the history of wicked popes and Neros? He assures us that Alexander VI, the worst and most impious man of his time, always succeeded in his schemes because he knew perfectly the weakness of men toward credulity. But I dare say that his success was not so much due to the credulity of men as to the circumstances and events which reacted to the advantage of the pope, such as the conflicting ambitions of the French and the Spanish, the disunity and hatred among the Italian ruling families, and the passions and weakness of Louis XII, all of which were contributing factors.

Deceit is likewise a flaw in political style when it is pushed too far. I will cite the authority of an able politician, Don Louis de Haro, who told Cardinal Mazarin that he had a significant political defect in that he always wanted to cheat. That same Mazarin wanted to employ Marshal de Fabert in a slippery negotiation, and the marshal said to him: "Allow me, Monseigneur, to refuse to betray the Duke of Savoy inasmuch as it is such a trifling thing, for it is known throughout the world that I am an honest man. Therefore, reserve the use of my integrity for a more important occasion when the safety of France is at stake."

At the moment I do not wish to speak further concerning the matters of virtue. But in the simple consideration of the princes' own interests I say that it is very poor politics on their part to be deceitful and to dupe the world, for they can succeed but once, and then they have lost the confidence of all princes. A certain ruler declares ultimately in a written manifesto the motives for his conduct, then he immediately proceeds in a manner directly opposite. I have noticed that such quick strokes soon alienate all confidence, for the greater the contradiction the quicker the retribution. In order to avoid an inconsistency of this kind, the Roman Church has very wisely decreed that all prospective saints undergo a noviciate of one hundred years, from the time they die, during which the memory of their mistakes and their extravagances disappear with them. The witnesses of their lives, therefore, having become extinct, and in the absence of evidence against them, there is no one to oppose their sanctification.

If I may be pardoned for that digression, I have noticed moreover that there are some unfortunate occasions when a prince should not be condemned for breaking his treaties and alliances. But in such cases he should part with his allies as an honest man, giving them ample notice of his intentions, and, above all, avoiding extreme measures that are not required by the urgency of the situation.

I shall finish this chapter with a single reflection. The fecundity with which the vices have been propagated by the hands of Machiavelli has been noted. He wants an incredulous king to crown his incredulity with hypocrisy. He thinks the people will be more impressed by the show of devotion than revolted by the bad treatment they have received from him. There are persons who hold to this sentiment, but as for me it seems that one ought always to have indulgence for the errors of speculation when they are not accompanied immediately by corruption of the heart, and that the people will have more affection for an incredulous prince — but an honest man who guards their welfare — than for an orthodox criminal and malefactor. For it is not the opinions of princes, but rather their actions, that make men blessed.

Machiavelli the Realist

MAX LERNER

Max Lerner, popular writer and teacher, has been professor of American Civilization and Political Institutions at Brandeis University since 1949, and a columnist for the *New York Post*. As a student of government and economics, and as an editor, writer, and teacher, Lerner has established a reputation for astute observation and crisp exposition of the many facets of modern life and politics. His published works are extensive, including such influential treatises as *It is Later than You Think* (1938); *Ideas Are Weapons* (1939); *Ideas for the Ice Age: Studies in a Revolutionary Era* (1941); and *America as a Civilization* (1957).

WHAT gives *The Prince* its greatness? It is not a great formal treatise on politics. It is bare of any genuine insights into social organization as the basis of politics. It has very little passion in it — so little that, because the final chapter crackles and glows with Machiavelli's fervor for the unification of Italy, some commentators have suggested that it is not an organic part of the book but was added as an after-thought. It has been pretty well proved, moreover, by recent scholarship that Machiavelli's little pamphlet on princes is not even original in form. It is part of a whole traditional literature on princes that stretches back to the Middle Ages. The structure of the book, its division into chapters and even some of the chapter headings follow the conventional form of what has been called the mirror-of-princes literature: the discussion of how to rule conquered territory, what advisers a prince should rely on, how he should conduct himself among the intrigues of diplomacy, whether he should depend mainly on fortified castles or entrenched camps in warfare.

But the intellectual spirit that pervades the book is quite another matter. Here we are in the presence of something little short of a revolution in political thinking. The humanists who had written books about princes had written in the idealistic and scholastic medieval tradition; they were ridden by theology and metaphysics. Machiavelli rejected metaphysics, theology, idealism. The whole drift of his work is toward a political realism, unknown to the formal writing of his time. . . .

He was able, using the traditional humanist literary forms, to pour into them a realistic political spirit which his age was acting on but which had never before been so well expressed in political thought. He had the daring to turn against the whole idealistic preoccupation of the humanists. He had the clear-eyed capacity to distinguish between man as he ought to be and man as he actually is — between the ideal form of institutions and the pragmatic conditions under which they operate.

But if we have come close to his greatness here, we have not wholly succeeded in ensnaring it. There have been other men who have expressed the consciousness of their period. They have in very few instances achieved the highest rank in the history of ideas. And while those who content themselves with seeing Machiavelli thus in the context of his time may succeed thereby in countering the charges made against him of being a sort of anti-Christ who had created a new immorality, they do not thereby get at the roots of his greatness. . . .

Machiavelli wrote a grammar of power, not only for the sixteenth century, but for the ages that have followed. Read *The Prince* today and you will be struck by the detonations which its sentences set off in the corridors of our experiences with present-day rulers. Machiavelli seen only in his historical context does become intelligible; but his greatness does not emerge until we see that when he wrote his grammar of power he came close to setting down the imperatives by which men govern and are governed in political communities, whatever the epoch and whatever the governmental structure.

The Prince has become, for better or worse, a symbol of a whole body of literature and a whole approach to politics. Just as in literature and art we must always face, under whatever names, the polar conflict of classic and romantic, so in the history of political thinking we have always to face the polar conflict between the ethical and the ruthlessly realistic. *The Prince* is part of the world's polemical literature because it places itself squarely in the ranks of realism. It brushes aside, with an impatience in which Machiavelli scarcely cares to conceal his disdain, the tender-mindedness of reformers and idealists.

There is in all of us, along with the ethical and normative strain, a strain of hard-headedness and of the acceptance of the framework of human passions and social reality within which we have to work. One can trace it back to Aristophanes and the way in which he always deflated contemporary dreams and illusions by getting back to the essential limits of the human animal. In every generation since him the young men have been divided between the pursuit of some passionate ideal and the hard-bitten inquiry into how things actually get accomplished in a real political world. It is to that pole of our political

thinking that *The Prince* gravitates. As long as this strain will remain in political thinking, so long will *The Prince* be found to have expressed in undying prose its intensity and its temper.

Very few who talk of *The Prince* have ever read more than a few sentences in it. But fewer still have read the work of Machiavelli which, without having the same *éclat* in history as *The Prince,* is nevertheless the saner, the more rounded, the more comprehensive work. I refer to *The Discourses.* . . .

What are the basic ideas of *The Discourses?* I should say the following: first, the superiority of the democratic republic to every other political form; second, the ultimate reliance even of despotic and authoritarian regimes on mass consent; third, the primary political imperative of cohesiveness, organic unity in a state, stability and survival; fourth, the great role of leadership (what Machiavelli calls the role of the lawgiver, but what we should today call leadership) in achieving this cohesiveness and survival; fifth, the imperative of military power in insuring survival and the need for putting it on a mass base (he felt that war was the health of the state); sixth, the use of a national religion for state purposes, and the choice of one not for its supernatural validity, but for its power as a myth in unifying the masses and cementing their morale (Machiavelli's count against Christianity, like that of Nietzsche after him, was that by glorifying humility and pacifism and the weaker virtues, it dulled the fighting edge of a state); seventh, the need in the conduct even of a democratic state for the will to survive, and therefore for ruthless instead of half-hearted measures when ruthless measures were necessary; eighth, the idea — later to be found in Vico and in our day in Spengler — of the cyclical rise and fall of civilizations due to the decadence and corruption of the old and the reinvigoration of the new.

This is, of course, only a sampling of the vast riches to be found in *The Discourses.* It is not a single-themed, monolithic book, such as Marx or Mill wrote. It has a catholicity and vastness of resource which will make it yield different discoveries for every reader and on every reading.

This is not the place to discuss the themes I have mentioned. I want only to say that if *The Prince* is great because of its intensity, *The Discourses* are great because of their variety; if *The Prince* is great because it is polemical, *The Discourses* are great because they have balance; and if *The Prince* is great because it gives us the grammar of power for a government, *The Discourses* are great because they give us the philosophy of organic unity not in a government but in a state, and the conditions under which alone a culture can survive. . . .

May I venture a guess as to the reason why we still shudder slightly at Machiavelli's name? It is not only the tradition I have described. It is our recognition that the realities he described *are* realities; that men, whether in politics, in business or in private life, do *not* act according to their professions of virtue; that leaders in every field seek power ruthlessly and hold on to it tenaciously; that the masses who are coerced in a dictatorship have to be wooed and duped in a democracy; that deceit and ruthlessness invariably crop up in every state; and that while the art of being ruled has always been a relatively easy one, the art of ruling ourselves is monstrously difficult. Machiavelli today confronts us with the major dilemma of how to adapt our democratic techniques and concepts to the demands of a world in which as never before naked power politics dominates the foreign field and determined oligarchies struggle for power internally. It is not an easy dilemma to resolve. And in a sense, just as the seventeenth- and eighteenth-century monarchs hated and feared Machiavelli because he had exposed their authority to the world, so today we hate and fear him because he has exposed our dilemma and made it visible to ourselves and the world.

Let us be clear about one thing: ideals and ethics are important in politics as norms, but they are scarcely effective as techniques. The successful statesman is an artist, concerned with nuances of public mood, approximations of operative motives, guesswork as to the tactics of his opponents, back-breaking work in unifying his own side by compromise and concession. Religious reformers have often succeeded in bringing public morale closer to some ethical norm; they have never succeeded as statesmen. Even in the theocracies of Savonarola in Florence, Cromwell and the Puritans in England, our own New England colonies, the men of God, when they came to power, learned to play the game of power. The only difference between them and others is that, since they had a certitude of having a pipeline to God, they did not have to reckon at all with the uneasy factor of their conscience. The most destructive imperialisms of the world have been those of men who have elevated their preferences to the pinnacle of moral imperatives and who have then confidently proceeded to impose those imperatives on others.

Today, as in Machiavelli's day, our world has become a collection of principalities struggling for survival, maneuvering for position, fighting over spoils. The scale is bigger but the proportions are the same. The strong men have come forward in every state, using the rhetoric of mass interest and national glory to extend their power and entrench their class. The first law of internal policy is to hold on to power, of external policy it is to extend your imperialism. Like Machiavelli, we live in a time of the breaking of nations.

Let it be said that Machiavelli in his day blundered as we are doing in ours. He could not make up his mind whether what he wanted was a democratic Florence or a unified Italy. I think he must have felt, when he wrote *The Prince,* that democracy would somehow follow if unity was achieved. There are some today who feel the same way about the attempts to achieve world integration through establishing a

Russian Century or an American Century. There are others who feel that no integration is worth the candle if democratic rights and human decencies are scrapped in the process. In Machiavelli's writing you will find both attitudes, but more often the first.

This raises sharply, of course, the interminable question of ends and means. Machiavelli would, I think, shrug his shoulders at the whole problem. He himself, he would say, was an observer of politics. And as such he would find it irrelevant to impose his own ethical patterns on the torrential flow of world history. It is for that very reason that Machiavellianism, after everything has been said about it, fails to be an adequate philosophy for a way of life. Men are not only observers, not only participants; they are also valuing individuals. Without judgment life loses its hierarchical quality of being a choice between preferences. And losing that, it loses its savor.

Machiavelli sought to distinguish the realm of what ought to be and the realm of what is. He rejected the first for the second. But there is a third realm: the realm of what can be. It is in that realm that what one might call a humanist realism can lie. The measure of man is his ability to extend this sphere of the socially possible. We can start with our democratic values, and we can start also with Machiavelli's realism about tough-minded methods. To be realistic about methods in the politics of a democracy at home does not mean that you throw away all scruples, or accept the superior force of "reason of state," or embrace the police-state crushing of constitutional liberties. To be realistic about the massing of power abroad in the economic and ideological struggle for the support of men and women throughout the world does not mean that you abandon the struggle for peace and for a constitutional imperium that can grow into a world republic. We may yet find that an effective pursuit of democratic values is possible within the scope of a strong social-welfare state and an unsentimental realism about human motives.

The Autonomy and Necessity of Politics

BENEDETTO CROCE

One of the most influential philosophers of history in the first half of the twentieth century was undoubtedly Benedetto Croce. Born in Abruzzi, Italy, in 1866, Croce was the leading contributor to what he called "ethico-political history" (a balance of history as politics and as art). Before his death in 1952 Croce's interests ranged widely over the fields of philosophy, aesthetics, and historiography, but he also took an active part in Italian politics, serving for many years in the Italian senate. As a liberal philosopher and critic of materialistic nationalism (also of Roman clericalism), Croce fought for a high standard of justice and achievement in Italian education, thought, and politics. From 1922 to 1924 he supported the Fascists, thinking they would infuse a new vigor and sensitivity into Italian life, but when he realized the danger and coarseness of the movement he quickly became its most outspoken opponent.

THE name of Machiavelli has become almost a symbol of politics in the real sense of the word, and it certainly marks a turning point in the history and development of the science. Not that antiquity did not have some suggestion of the distinction and the contradiction between politics and ethics; the very fact that their content was attributed to two diverse disciplines proves that such an attitude did exist; and debates such as those over just and unjust rights, over genuine and conventional laws, and also over force and justice, likewise show how the contradiction could sometimes be averted and the problem correlated when it was guarded against. But that contradiction never again rose to top importance and did not become the center of contention and of thought. And not even during the long centuries of the domination of Christian thought did this change, for the contrast between the City of God and the City of Man, and then between the Church and the Empire, found its own composition in the doctrine of the double rule instituted by God — or even in the supremacy of the Church over the Empire or the Empire over the Church — but it did not become sharpened by speculative dissension. Yet there was no doubt that Christian thought, which had such a part in the inquiry into the moral conscience, refined this conscience and prepared it for the dissension which was sure to burst forth. Niccolò Machiavelli is considered to be a genuine expression of the Italian Renaissance; but at the same time he was certainly connected in some ways to the Reformation movement by the general need which was revived in that age, both in Italy and outside as well, to know man and to search out the problems of the soul.

It is well known that Machiavelli discovered the necessity and the autonomy of politics, politics which is beyond good and bad morals, which has its own laws against which it is futile to rebel, which cannot be exorcised and banished from the world with holy water. This is the conception that circulates in all of his works and which, although not formulated there with that

From Benedetto Croce, *Elementi di politica*. (Bari: Gius. Laterza & Figli, 1925), pp. 59–67. Reprinted by permission of the publishers. Translated by the editor.

didactical and scholastical accuracy which has usually come to take the place of philosophy, and although its presence there is also disturbed sometimes by fantastic images, by figures that oscillate between political virtue and villainy for ambitions of power, nevertheless is a conception profoundly philosophical, and represents the true and proper foundation for a philosophy of politics.

But that which usually is not observed is the sharp bitterness with which Machiavelli accompanies this assertion about politics and about its intrinsic necessity. "If men were all good" (he says), "these precepts would not be good." But men are "ungrateful, variable, fugitives from danger, greedy for profit"; so that one ought to think rather of making himself feared than loved, procuring first the fear and later, if possible, the love. It is necessary to learn "to be bad"; to keep faith when you govern, but not always, for otherwise men will surely take advantage of you; to destroy whoever watches for a good moment to destroy you. The desire of Machiavelli goes out to an unattainable society of good and pure people, and he fancies such a society in the distant past, but meanwhile he prefers the less cultured people to the more cultured, those of Germany and the mountaineers of Switzerland to the Italians, French, and Spaniards (then in their zenith), who were the "corruption of the world." Whoever reads about the horrors that history tells us "will without doubt, if he is born of man, be dismayed by every imitation of wicked times, and will kindle a great desire to follow the good." (Such is the sentiment that he demonstrates and loudly declares.) In the face of such open indications of an austere and painful moral awareness, it is amazing that there should still be so much talk about the immorality of Machiavelli; except that what the lower classes call moral is only moralistic pretense and devotional hypocrisy. The lack of that bitter sentiment and pessimism is what distinguishes Guicciardini from Machiavelli. Guicciardini demonstrates

nothing other than a kind of contempt toward men in whom so "little goodness" is discovered, and who is so peacefully comfortable in this worthless world watching out only for his own "personal" advantage. If it were not for this "personal" self, he would not have served the Medici popes, and would have thought "more of Martin Luther than of himself," for he would have expected that the rebellious friar could break up the ecclesiastical state and ruin the "wicked tyranny of the clergy." Guicciardini's man is of a different mettle than the man of Machiavelli.

More important still is that Machiavelli should be almost divided in spirit and mind over the politics in which he had discovered autonomy and which appeared to him at times as an unfortunate necessity to have to dirty his own hands with, in order to deal with those who would live as beasts. Yet at other times politics seemed more like a sublime art for building and sustaining that great institution which is the state. Very often he speaks of it in a religious tone, as when he remembers the saying that it is necessary for the good of the state to be ready to give up not only one's reputation but the safety of the soul itself; or when he refers back with a little secret envy to the pagan religion, which placed the greatest good in the honor of the world and which exalted men who were filled with human glory and esteemed the grandeur of the soul, the strength of the body, and all the virtues which surround men of great force and vitality. In contrast is the Christian religion, with its demonstrations of truth and the sure way to the other world, with its scorn for this world, its praise of misery and of the visionary men who exalt the former above the latter, and which places "enduring" above "doing."

Is politics diabolical or divine? Machiavelli regarded it in the image of the centaur — which the poets precisely depicted as a beautiful thing between human and animal — and described his prince as half man and half beast; and so there would be no doubt about the fullness of the human part, he even provided it with mental arguments, wickedness, and the rejection of the beast-like part, desiring that the latter might be between the fox and the lion — because the lion cannot protect itself from the snares and the fox cannot defend itself against the wolves — for it would be like a novice in the art of ruling to want "to always be like the lion." The art and science of politics — that of pure politics — brought to maturity by Italians, were the object of much pride to him, so that when the cardinal of Rohan told him that Italians did not understand war, he responded that "the French do not understand the state."

The successor of Machiavelli does not need to be sought either among the Machiavellians, who continue with his casuistry and rhetorical politics and write about "reason of state," often mixing it with their own trivial moralistic precepts; nor among the anti-Machiavellians, proclaimers of the fusion and identification of politics with morality and idealizers of the states constructed on the pure dictates of goodness and justice; nor among the eclectics, who put into juxtaposition the theory of morality and the theory of politics, and, instead of resolving the contradiction, they confuse it and experiment with it, turning it into the misfortunes and dissensions which befall the world but which are re-clothed as accidental things. The successor of Machiavelli was indeed another Italian (and certainly in these two Italians the philosophy of politics can be clearly symbolized in its essence), Vico, who was not particularly kind to Machiavelli, but who was full of his spirit, which he clarifies and purifies, integrating his concept of politics and history, compounding his doubts and exhilarating his pessimism.

For Vico, politics, force, the creative energy of the state, becomes a moment of the human spirit and of the life of society, an eternal moment, the moment of certainty which continues forever, through dialectical unfolding, the moment of truth, of reason completely clarified through justice and morality, or through ethics. The

symbol of the centaur shows itself to be inadequate after all: that which formerly seemed to be the savage part of man unveils itself also as human, the highest form of the human will, the foundation of all others. Without passions, without force, without authority humanity does not rise; the strong men are the best, and by the continuation then of the dominion of the strong, a noble society comes forth and the citizens which they rule form a contrast; yet nevertheless, without such a generous barbarity humanity could not be. And in that barbarity society combines to be re-tempered in the same way that Machiavelli used to say that the states should be called back to their principles from time to time, generalizing the saying of the Florentines who professed to convene every five years "to reprimand the state," that is, "to put that same terror and fear into the men which they had caused when seizing the state." Thus, whereas Machiavelli in dealing with the art of the state became religious, Vico never hesitated to speak of the "divinity of force"; and, like Machiavelli, who found that the most pliable to the touch of the political hand were "the men of the mountains where no civilization had reached" — for a sculptor forms a beautiful statue more easily from a piece of virgin marble than from another statue already rough hewn" — so also did Vico see in the barbarian people a more vigorous political vitality, which generates more easily than from other new states, where the people are badly civilized and corrupted and cannot be reformed. The poorly hewn and wasted statue must be reset in the caldron in order to cast it again. The hardness and the treachery, inevitable in politics and which Machiavelli recognized and recommended, though occasionally experiencing moral nausea, are to be explained by Vico as part of the drama of humanity which is perpetually being created and recreated. . . .

Such is the unconscious Vicoism of Machiavelli and the involuntary Machiavellism of Vico — which is not found clearly formulated in what they wrote, but which can be gathered from their scattered concepts, from their judgments, parallelisms, divergencies, etc. — that is manifested to the expert eye of anyone who has followed the development of their thought and their lives, and which has become, for that reason, more comprehensible than they themselves might have been able to realize.

MACHIAVELLI THE PATRIOT

The Regeneration of Italy

PASQUALE VILLARI

> Pasquale Villari (1827–1917), like Croce, was an eminent Neapolitan scholar-politician. From his early years he took an active part in the agitation for Italian unification, and participated in the May 1848 revolt in Naples. He was a professor of history at Pisa and at the Institute of Higher Studies in Florence, became a member of the national Council of Education in 1862, and later was Under Secretary of State for Education. In 1884 he entered the senate and then served as Minister of Education. In addition to other historical works, Villari wrote two books which have almost become classics: *The Life and Times of Girolamo Savonarola*, 2 vols. (1859–61); and *The Life and Times of Niccolò Machiavelli*, 2 vols. (1877–82), both of which were translated into English by his wife.

MACHIAVELLI, as we have seen, was very closely connected with his times. Therefore our estimate of him must greatly depend upon our estimate of the age in which he lived. He came into the world at a moment when political corruption was general throughout Europe, but more predominant in Italy than elsewhere on account of the greater number of persons taking part in public life. Hence the evil effects of this corruption infected every section of society in our country. Our culture enhanced the criminality of the vices and misdeeds of a statecraft no longer ruled by the blind and ungoverned passions of the Middle Ages, but the product of refined calculation and cunning, full of cruelty and devoid of scruples. With us, mediaeval institutions rapidly fell into decay, leaving individual members of the community deprived of all guidance save that of their own instincts. In France, England, and Spain, feudalism still served as a basis for the sovereign power of those three great monarchies. But, possessed of more stable traditions, they were compelled to pursue a policy that, while no less corrupt as regarded its means, was necessarily more national in its aims. . . .

Without having extensive culture, Machiavelli early learnt to prize Pagan antiquity more highly than all else, and had a particular admiration for the Romans. His mind was formed by their history and their literature. Nature had gifted him with an extraordinarily limpid and acute intelligence; with an exquisite taste for elegance of form, with a most lively fancy, which although insufficient to make him a poet, influenced him continually; with a mordant and satiric spirit discerning the comic side of human events, and giving added force to the pungent wit of the sarcastic sallies that gained him so many enemies and detractors. For he had a kindly nature, and cannot be charged with a

From Pasquale Villari, *The Life and Times of Niccolò Machiavelli*, translated by Linda Villari, (London: 2 vols., Ernest Benn Ltd., 1929), II. 509, 511–517. Reprinted by permission of the publishers.

17

single bad action. His manners were certainly loose, but less so than might be imagined from the very licentious language which, according to the custom of the day, he adopted in his letters and his plays. Toward his wife and children he showed unvarying affection to the last hour of his existence. But Machiavelli's real life was all in his intellect: therein lay the true source of his greatness. His predominating mental gift, and that in which he outstripped all his contemporaries, was a singular power of piercing to the innermost kernel of historic and social facts. He was no patient investigator of minute historical details, nor had he the speculative genius required to dwell upon metaphysical and abstract considerations touching the nature of man. But he was unequalled in exploring and bringing to light the first origin and special result of any political revolution or social transformation. He was unequalled in discerning the qualities determining the nature of a people or a state. Nor could any one rival him in the power of indicating what was the character in any given society, not so much of this or that sovereign in particular, as of the sovereign, captain, aristocracy or people in general. It was in these things that all the mighty originality of his intelligence was shown.

And it was this predominant faculty that gave him so irresistible a vocation for a life devoted to public affairs. Not that it was a career leading him to wealth, since, despite his great aptitude for business, he was not possessed in any exceptional degree of that practical intuition of individual character conferring the instinctive power of guiding and mastering men. In this gift he was surpassed by many of his contemporaries, and notably by Guicciardini. Nevertheless, Machiavelli found in public affairs a wide field for the exercise of his observant faculty, and for his feverish activity of mind, and was accordingly passionately devoted to them. On first assuming the Secretaryship of the Republic he was merely an excellent official servant. But his assiduity in his duties, his aptitude

for planning and originating new designs, gained him the confidence of Soderini, who speedily began to employ him in matters of greater moment.

The circumstance that decided once for all the direction of his future studies, set him on the road for which he was naturally predestined, and formed the commencement of his true political training, was his mission to the court of the Duke of Valentinois. He then perceived how an adventurer of the worst type, and capable of the most iniquitous actions, might yet have grand qualities as a statesman and general. By a course of bloodshed and treason the duke actually succeeded in extirpating the most abominable tyrants of Romagna. He founded a government that re-established order, tranquility, and prompt administration of justice among the hardy inhabitants of that province, who once delivered from oppression, began to prosper, and conceived a lively affection for their new ruler. Had he been a kinder, or less corrupt man, had he shown any hesitation, his mercy, so Machiavelli thought, would have been cruel. The figure of Caesar Borgia rose before his eyes as the living personification of the moral contrast afflicting the age, and helped him to explain the enigma. He clearly saw that statecraft has ways and means of its own, which are not the ways and means of private morality; that, on the contrary, the morality of private life may sometimes check a statesman in mid-career and render him vacillating, without his being either a good or a bad man; and that it is mainly vacillation of this kind that leads to the downfall of States. There must be no vacillation, he said, but a daring adoption of the measures demanded by the nature of events. Such measures will always be justified, when the end is obtained. And the end in view must be the welfare of the State. He who achieves this, even if a wicked man, may be condemned for his wickedness, but will deserve, as a prince, everlasting glory. If, on the contrary, he should cause the ruin of the State, whether through private ambition, or from hesitation born of a good motive, he will be consigned to infamy as a wicked or incapable prince, even when, as a private individual, deserving the highest praise. Such is the true meaning of Machiavelli's maxim: that the end justifies the means. . . .

The fall of the Republic was a personal misfortune, inasmuch as it deprived him of office, drove him from public affairs, and plunged him in the greatest financial difficulties; nevertheless, it proved a blessing in disguise, since it forced him to think and to write, and won him immortality. Had he always preserved his secretaryship, we should have had nothing from his pen excepting the "Legazioni." But on being condemned to private life, his ideas began to assume shape and order; his mental horizon to widen. The Medici being all-powerful in Rome and Florence, it was impossible at that time to hope for the revival of popular government, and he therefore began to meditate on the constitution of a strong Italian State. He thus invented his political system, which has a double character. On the one hand, he gives us a new science of Statesmanship; on the other, he continually applies this science to the Italy of his own day, and seeks practical methods of erecting her into a nation, and putting her on the road to real greatness. This duplex conception was expounded in the "Prince," the "Discourses," and the "Art of War," and is more or less evident throughout all Machiavelli's works. Equally duplex, too, is the basis of his system, for it is founded upon experience and the lessons of history, the latter being nearly always brought in to support the conclusions of the former.

In the "Histories" we find Machiavelli inspired by the same Republican spirit by which we have beheld him dominated amid the whirl of affairs, and to which he was unceasingly faithful. In penning his "Histories" he thought to have discovered that all great political events were the invariable product of the will and intelligent daring of some great man. He became convinced that the ruin of Italy was the direct result of her divisions and of the foreign invasions principally caused by Papal greed.

Our Italian motherland, he said in conclusion, can never be prosperous nor great until it is united, and its unity can only be the work of a Prince-reformer. This prince always appeared to him in the likeness of Caesar Borgia, as a strong and intelligent will, capable of organizing and disorganizing, making and unmaking nations at his own pleasure. This incarnated will-power is almost a natural force, foregoing all personal characteristics, all individual and moral value; it becomes one with its deeds, by which, and by the end accomplished is it alone to be judged. And only to a solitary directing will is it given to establish and organize the State. The people may be able to preserve and develop it, to ensure its prosperity, but can never be its creator.

In this strain the "Prince" was conceived and written. It lays before us the constitution and organization of a State by the work of the man who is its living personification, but in whom the individual and private conscience is, as it were, eradicated. The prince must override every obstacle to the accomplishment of his great purpose; must be checked by no scruples. It was in this way that the mind of Machiavelli gradually wrought out his conception of the organic unity of the State, and it was in the same way that the modern State afterwards took shape in real history. This demonstrates the great value of his conception, and explains the singular fascination it has exercised, all calumnies notwithstanding, upon the minds of thinkers and politicians. It was the scientific character of the work that led the author to examine with equal indifference both the virtuous and the wicked prince, and offer to either the counsels suited to the achievement of his end. These counsels are the outcome of earnest study of actual events, of ancient and modern history, without any reference to moral considerations. The *case of conscience,* so unavoidably present to our own minds, never seems to occur to that of Machiavelli, who is solely concerned in inquiring which

is the road to power, and how the State is
to be established. He never puts himself
the question: whether the excessive immorality of the means employed, may not, even
while momentarily grasping the desired
end, sap the very foundations of society,
and render in the long run all good and
strong government an impossibility. He
forgets to inquire whether, just as there is
a private morality, there may not be also a
social and political morality, imposing certain inviolable limits, and furnishing rules
for the statesman's conduct, which, although varying with the times and different
social conditions, are yet equally subject to
righteous principles. This is the weak and
fallacious side of his doctrine; that which
disgusts us with its author, arouses our
horror, and has been a perennial source of
accusation and calumny.

But when, on completing his analysis,
and cruel labour of vivisection, Machiavelli
proceeds to draw his conclusions, then at
last the practical side and real aim of his
work are clearly seen. It is a question of
achieving the unity of his Italian motherland and of delivering it from foreign rule.
This was certainly the holiest of objects;
but Machiavelli well knew that in the
conditions in which Italy and Europe were
then involved it would be impossible to
achieve that object without recurring to the
immoral means practised by the statesmen
of the time. Pursued by this idea, and
dominated by his theme, Machiavelli did
not pause to disentangle the scientific, general, and permanent aim of his book from
the practical aim and transitory means, apparently and, it may be, really essential to
its achievement at that moment. It is need-
ful, he said in conclusion, to dare all things,
and in view of the grandeur and sacredness
of the end, to yield to no scruples. Solely
by the formation of a united, powerful, and
independent nation can Italy acquire liberty, virtue, and true morality. This is an
enterprise only to be undertaken by a
Prince-reformer, and by the means suggested and imposed by history and experience. The people must afterwards complete

and consolidate it by liberty, by national
arms, by public and private virtue.

It is this second idea that forms the special theme of the "Discourses." They start
from the same conception as that of the
"Prince"; some one man must be the
founder of the State, and go forward relent-
lessly to his end. They then proceed to
show how the people should possess itself
of the government, render it strong and
prosperous, and administer it by means of
free institutions and morality. And here,
with an inexhaustible fund of just, profound, and practical observations, the
author lays the basis of a new science of
statesmanship. We must, however, confine
ourselves to remarking that the whole literature of the fifteenth and sixteenth centuries contains no other pages in any way
comparable with those of the "Discourses"
in praise of the love of liberty, patriotic
devotion, and the sacrifice of all private interest to the public good. For there, as in
the exhortation at the close of the "Prince,"
Machiavelli's patriotism is vented with an
eloquence bordering upon sublimity. At
such moments his character gains elevation
in our eyes, his figure assumes heroic proportions, and still more so when we remember that his patriotism not only inspired his
intellect, but guided the conduct of his
entire life.

To have freedom, the people must also
have strength, and therefore Machiavelli
was led to write his "Art of War." This
work shows that, during the Pisan war, and
throughout his various travels, he must
have devoted much inquiry to the organization of foreign armies, for the sole purpose of discovering a means of regenerating
the Italian arms, and was thus enabled to
arrive at thoroughly original conclusions.
For these studies not only led to the conception of his "Ordinanza," of the armed
nation, but likewise caused him to recognize and proclaim that the genuine strength
of armies, as of nations, consists in virtue.
Without virtue, he concluded, a people can
neither be strong nor free; can never ac-
complish anything great. The training of

Italians to arms, to constant readiness to give their lives and their all for their country, can alone constitute the real beginning of their regeneration. And where, we may once more repeat, are other writings to be found extolling virtue with the heat or earnestness so nobly and eloquently poured forth in the "Art of War"?

Nor were these phrases mere empty rhetoric. The best years of Machiavelli's life, his whole stock of energy and persistent, irrepressible activity, were dedicated to realizing the ideas expounded in this work. It is impossible not to grant him our admiration when we find him preaching the necessity of arming the people, training it to self-sacrifice for its country's cause, and ceaselessly endeavouring to impress Soderini and the Republic of Florence with the same conviction. Nor was he content with this alone. We find him in his days of misfortune and persecution at the hands of the Medici, recommencing the same propaganda among the youthful band of the Oricellarii Gardens. Again later, when of advanced age and shaken health, we see him, forgetful of himself and his own private interests, endeavouring to convert even Clement VII to his ideas. And his promptitude in offering to be the first initiator of the noble attempt, at the terrible time when the hosts of Charles V were already advancing to overwhelm Italy in ruin, actually infused a momentary spark of enthusiasm into the Pope's uncertain soul. We are then forced to acknowledge that Machiavelli had at least one great and heroic passion redeeming, elevating and raising him above all his contemporaries: an ardent and irresistible love for liberty, his country, and even for virtue. And in remembering this, the brows of him who has been so persistently stigmatized as the incarnation of evil

and moral darkness, become suddenly crowned with a divine splendour that glorifies the age.

This, then, was the process followed by Machiavelli's mind throughout his various works. Taken one by one, their unity fails to strike us, their aim is lost sight of, and they give occasion for the strangest misinterpretations and calumnies. Taken as a whole, we not only comprehend their value, but discern the path pursued by the national idea — then the idea of the age — personified in the great Florentine, in order to escape from the labyrinth of contradictions in which it was involved.

Italy had become incapable of a religious reformation similar to that accomplished in Germany. Instead of springing toward God, as Savonarola had predicted; instead of seeking strength in a new conception of faith, she aimed at a re-composition of the idea of the State and the motherland. She saw in the sacrifice of all to the universal good the only possible way of political and moral redemption. The unity of the regenerated country would have inevitably led to the re-establishment of morality, would have rekindled faith in public and private virtue, and discovered a method of sanctifying the purpose of life. This idea, vaguely and feebly felt by many, was the ruling thought of Machiavelli, the shrine upon which he offered up his entire existence. His dying eyes beheld the spectacle of Italy's ruin. Afterwards his great thought remained a dream, and he was therefore the least understood and most calumniated personality that history has known.

At the present day, when Italy's political redemption has begun, and the nation is constituted according to the prophecies of Machiavelli, the moment has at last come for justice to be done to him.

Long Live Italian Unity: Glory to Machiavelli!

FRANCESCO DE SANCTIS

The first Neapolitan scholar-statesman to establish himself in the top rank of thinkers, artists, and politicians was Francesco De Sanctis (1817–1883). De Sanctis has been called the greatest nineteenth century student of Italian literature, and is usually recognized as the founder of modern literary criticism in Italy. From his youth De Sanctis had been active in education and letters, and when Garibaldi overran southern Italy in 1859 he made De Sanctis Minister of Education in Naples. Cavour chose him as education minister for the newly united Italy, and subsequently De Sanctis served in several cabinets. As professor of comparative literature at the University of Naples, his influence on Italian writers was great. Among his many notable students was Villari himself.

MACHIAVELLI lived in the world of the Renaissance, and he also participated in it. He took life with the same license, and theory with the same indifference, as the men of his times. His cultural level was not extremely high; many of his contemporaries were ahead of him — and of Ariosto, too — in learning and erudition. Nor did philosophical speculations seem to impress him any more than did scholastic and theological arguments. At any rate, he paid no attention to them. His spirit was devoted entirely to the practical life.

Nor does Machiavelli seem to be very well informed on matters of natural science when we see in his writings the references to the influence of the stars. Certainly Battista Alberti possessed a much broader and more refined culture. But Niccolò was not a philosopher of nature, he was a philosopher of man. And in this his genius surpassed rationalism and prepared the way for Galileo.

Man, as Machiavelli conceives him, does not have the ecstatic and contemplative face of the Middle Ages, nor the tranquil and idyllic face of the Renaissance. He has the modern face of a man who works and builds toward a goal.

Every man has his mission on earth, according to his aptitudes. Life is neither a touch of the imagination nor a matter of contemplation. It is not theology and is not even art. It has its meaning here on earth as well as its purpose and means. To regain the earthly life, to give it direction, to revive consciousness, to recreate that inner strength, to restore earnestness and activity to mankind; this is the spirit which activates all the works of Machiavelli.

Machiavelli rejects the Middle Ages, and at the same time he denies the Renaissance. Divine meditation satisfies him about as little as does artistic contemplation. Culture and art are nice, but are not things that should, or could, constitute the object of life itself. He resists imagination as the most dangerous enemy of all, for to see a thing as it is imagined to be rather than as it really is, seems to him to be the malady in greatest need of a cure. He repeats everywhere that things need to be judged as they are and not as they ought to be. That "ought to be" tendency which pervades medieval content and Renaissance form, must give way to what "is," or, as he says, to the "effectual" truth.

Subordination of the imaginary world,

From Francesco de Sanctis, *Storia della letteratura italiana*, (Milan: Feltrinelli Editore, 1956), Vol. II, pp. 113–14, 116–17, 125–29, 153–55, 157. By permission of the publishers. Translated by the editor.

such as religion and art, to the real world, that is to experience and observation, is the true aim of Machiavelli.

After having rejected all of the supernatural and superhuman elements, he then proceeds to establish the *patria* as the foundation of existence. Man's mission in this life, and his first duty, is patriotism toward the glory, greatness, and liberty of the fatherland. . . .

To Machiavelli country was a divinity, superior even to morality and law. Just as the God of the ascetics absorbed the individual in himself, and in the name of God the inquisitors burned heretics; so for one's fatherland anything was lawful, and actions which in private life are crimes become magnanimous when done for the sake of country. "Reason of State" and "public welfare" were the common banners by which this right of the fatherland was considered superior to all other rights. God had descended from heaven to earth and called himself the *"patria,"* and he was no less terrible than before. The will and interests of fatherland were the "supreme law." The individual was always absorbed in the collective being, and when this collective being was itself absorbed into the will of a single person or a small group of persons, servitude was the result. Liberty was the participation, to a greater or lesser degree, of the citizens in public affairs. The rights of man did not yet intervene in the code of liberty. Man was not an autonomous being or an end in himself; he was an instrument of the country, or what was worse, of the state (a word meaning any kind of government, even that of a despot founded on the arbitrary will of one man). Country was where all took some part in governing, where all obeyed and all commanded; in other words, a "republic." When one man gave the orders and the rest obeyed it was called a "principality." But whether a republic or principality, a country or state, the conception was always that of the individual absorbed by society, or as they referred to it then, the omnipotence of the state.

These ideas are put forth by Machiavelli not as though they were discovered and analyzed by him, but as accepted through ancient tradition and strengthened by classical culture. They are filled with the spirit of ancient Rome, whose image of glory and of liberty attracted the imagination of everyone, for Rome was not only the model for art and literature, but for government as well.

The *patria* absorbed even religion. A state could not exist without religion. This is why Machiavelli grieved over the Roman court, for not only had it turned over the defense of its temporal domain to foreigners, but because of its disorderly and licentious customs had greatly reduced the authority of religion among the populace. What he wanted was a state religion which in the hands of the prince could be used as a means of governing. Thus religion had lost its true meaning and become an art to the literary world and an instrument of politics to the statesman. But morality also pleased Machiavelli, and he praised such things as generosity, clemency, keeping of the faith, sincerity, and the other virtues on the condition that they benefited the country — and when he encountered them in his way not as instruments for the improvement of the government but as obstacles to it, he broke them. His writings have many praises for the religion and other virtues of good princes; yet these passages always have a savor of rhetoric, which stands out even more boldly in the bareness of his prose. Neither in Machiavelli nor in his contemporaries is there a genuine and simple religious and moral sentiment.

*   *   *

Along with the decline of the scholastic form came the fall of the literary form based on a period of time. In didactic works the period served as a form of concealed syllogism, a proposition composed of its "major" and secondary premises (called "demonstration" when the material was intellectual, and "description" when it was pure facts). Machiavelli gives us simple propositions stripped of all embellishments; he does not describe or demonstrate, but merely narrates or states — and without recourse to the period artifice. Not only does he dispense with the classical literary form, but he completely throws out form itself (and this in an age of form, the only divinity still recognized). This is precisely his motive, for his mind is filled with a new content, a content which for him is everything and the form nothing. Or to say it more correctly, the form itself is the thing in its effectual truth, that is in its intellectual or material existence. . . .

The ornamentations of Boccaccio and Cicero had become conventionalized into a mechanism based entirely upon imitation in which the intellect itself remained a stranger. Philosophers had not yet left their scholastic form; poets still followed Petrarch; prose writers made use of a bastard genre, part poetical and part rhetorical, with an outward imitation of Boccaccio. But these were all symptoms of the same malady: passiveness or complete indifference of the intellect, of the heart, of the imagination, in short, of the whole spirit. Here were writers, but they were not men. Their only goal was to write as an occupation, a trade which consisted in a mechanism called "literary form," with the soul completely indifferent to anything else. The divorce between the man and the writer was complete. Amid all this rage of rhetorical writing appeared the prose of Machiavelli, the first suggestion of modern prose.

Here the man is everything, not as a writer, but only as a man. Machiavelli seems almost to ignore that there is such a thing as an art of writing — generally admitted to be a changing style or convention. Sometimes he does try it and proves himself a master; when he wants to even he can become a man of letters. Still the man is everything in him. Whatever he writes is an immediate product of his brain, flowing forth warm and fresh from within, thing and impression often condensed into a single word. For here is a man who thinks and feels, who destroys and creates, who observes and reflects, with his spirit always active and alert. He searches for the thing itself, not its color, and the thing comes forth from his brain pure and complete with its own impressions, therefore naturally colored, mixed with irony, melancholy, indignation, and dignity, yet mostly in its own plastic clarity. Machiavelli's prose is clear and full like marble, but marble with colorful lines in it. It has the grand style of Dante giving it life. When speaking of the changes which the Middle Ages introduced in the names of things and people, Machiavelli concludes: "From Caesars and Pompeys men likewise became Peters, Johns, and Matthews." Here nothing is seen but the marble, the bare thing; but how many veins there are in that marble! We feel all the impressions cut into the imagination of his brain: admiration for the Caesars and Pompeys, scorn for the Peters and Matthews, indignation over the change; and he is seen choosing the characteristic names and placing them in contrast like enemies, and in that final and energetic "they became," seems to say that the change was not just in name but in spirit and soul.

This prose, dry, precise, and concise, so filled with thought and matter, reveals an intellect already mature, emancipated from all traces of mysticism, ethics, and poetry, and coming to dominate the world; logic or the power of things [as distinguished from ideas], the modern fate. This is, in effect, the real meaning of the world as Machiavelli conceives it. Regardless of its origin, the world is what it is, a concentration of human and natural forces endowed with their own laws. The thing we call "fate" is nothing more than logic; the necessary result of these forces, appetites, instincts, passions, opinions, fantasies, interests, and maneuvers is the domination of a superior force, the human spirit, thought and intellect. The God of Dante is love, the uniting force of the intellect and the deed, whose end result is wisdom. The God of Machiavelli is the intellect; intelligence and the rule of the world force; the result is science.

"We must love," says Dante. "We must understand," says Machiavelli. The soul of Dante's world is the heart: the soul of Machiavelli's world is the brain. The former is essentially mystical and ethical; the latter is primarily human and logical. Virtue has changed its meaning with Machiavelli. It no longer means moral feeling, but simply force or energy, the mettle of the soul. Cesare Borgia is virtuous because he has the force to act according to logic, that is, accepting the means necessary to achieve the accepted end. Since the soul of Machiavelli's world is the brain, his prose is likewise nothing but brain. . . .

*   *   *

Machiavelli has formal logic and he also has content.

His logic has seriousness of purpose as its foundation, that which he calls *"virtù."* To propose an aim which one knows cannot be reached is feminine. "To be a man" means "to drive towards a goal." But often men go astray in their quest for a goal because their mind and will are confused by imagination and emotions, and they are led by appearances rather than realities. They are weak and feeble spirits who, like the masses, esteem things as they appear rather than as they are. To dispel all vain apparitions, and walk toward one's goal with clearness of mind and firmness of will, this is to be a man, to have the mettle of a man. This man may be a tyrant, or he may be a citizen, a good man or a wretch. But this is beside the point and has to do with another aspect of man. What Machiavelli is looking for is to see whether or not it is a man; his intention is to reactivate the wilting roots of the plant known as "man." In this logic of Machiavelli's, virtue is character, or mettle, and vice is incoherence, fear, and indecision.

It should be understood that this generalization contains lessons for everyone, the good as well as the bad, and the same book which seems to one person to be a code of tyranny, will appear as a code of freedom to another. What it teaches you is to be a man; this is the basis of everything else. It teaches that history, just like nature, is not determined by chance, but by intelligent and measurable forces which are based on the harmony between the end and the means; and that man, as a social being or as an individual, is not worthy of the name if he is not also an intelligent force, consistent with the end and means. Upon this foundation the virile age of the world is built, delivered perhaps from the influence of imaginations and passions, by a clear and serious goal and a precise and straightforward means.

This is the fundamental concept, the objective of Machiavelli. Yet it is not an abstract and idle principle: it is one with content, which we have just outlined in brief.

The seriousness of earthly life with its tool, work; with its objective, country; with its principle, equality and liberty; with its moral bond, the nation; with its agent, the spirit or thought of man — immutable and immortal; with its organization, the state — autonomous and independent; with the discipline of force; with justice for the interests of all; this is what is absolute and permanent in the world of Machiavelli; and by which it is crowned in glory (i.e., the approval of mankind), and given a foundation of virtue or character: *"agere et pati fortia."*

The scientific foundation of this world is the effectual thing, as offered by experience and observation. Imagination, sentiment, and abstraction are things pernicious to science, just as they are to life. When scholasticism dies, science is born.

This is true Machiavellism, alive, indeed even young. It is the program of the modern world, developed, corrected, amplified, and more or less realized. It is the great nations of the world that came closest to its realization. Let us therefore be proud of our Machiavelli. Glory to him whenever a part of the ancient edifice crumbles! And glory to him when some new part is added. Even as I am now writing these lines [1870] the bells are ringing throughout the land announcing the entry of the Italians into Rome. The temporal power is falling. The shout arises, "Long live Italian unity!" Glory to Machiavelli!

As a writer Machiavelli is not only profound, but also likeable. In his political transactions his real inclinations can always be discerned: anti-papal, anti-imperial, anti-feudal, civilized, modern, and democratic. And when we find him, eyes fixed on his goal, setting forth his arguments, frequently interrupting himself to protest, he seems to be asking for forgiveness and saying: Remember, that I am living in corrupt times, and if the methods are like this and the world acts this way, it is not my fault. . . .

Machiavellism, in final substance, is the considering of man as an autonomous and self-sufficient being who has within his own nature the end and the means (the laws of his development) for achieving his own greatness and his decadence, either as an individual or as a part of society. This is the original and fundamental basis of history, politics, and all of the social sciences. The beginnings of science are the portraits, discourses, and observations of men of classical culture with great experience and with clear and free intellects. This is Machiavellism both as a science and as a method. Here modern thought finds its foundation and its language. As for content, Machiavellism outlived a conscious and intentional world on the ruins of the Middle Ages; a world visible through the transactions and the vacillations of political man; a world founded upon country, nationality, liberty, equality, work, virility, and the earnestness of man.

A Sixteenth-Century Cavour

SIR RICHARD LODGE

One of the most distinguished English scholars of the early twentieth century was Sir Richard Lodge (1855–1936), whose painstaking scholarship and amicable teaching have had widespread influence. Lodge received his education at Oxford University, where he remained as a lecturer and tutor of Brasenose College. In 1894 he was appointed first Professor of Modern History at the University of Glasgow, and then in 1899 he accepted the chair at Edinburgh which he retained until his retirement in 1925. Lodge's studies were directed principally into the areas of the Renaissance, and eighteenth-century diplomatic history. He was knighted in 1917 for his academic and public services, and between 1929 and 1933 was president of the Royal Historical Society. The article which follows is his noteworthy presidential address before that society in February, 1930.

Few names are so familiar as that of Machiavelli, who has given at least an adjective to every European language, and few books have been subjected to such intense scrutiny and such industrious commentary as his most impressive work, *The Prince*. It may well be thought that there is nothing more to be said about either the author or the book, and that an apology is needed for adding even an ephemeral address to the enormous mass of literature about Machiavelli. My apology or explanation is a simple one. The great majority of the critics and commentators deal with problems which are of great interest in themselves but do not concern my immediate object. One of these is the ethical question as to how far the supposed interest of the state — the *raison d'état* — justifies a departure from the ordinary accepted canons of morality or honesty. Another is the place of Machiavelli in the history of what is called Political Science. And a third very fruitful topic is the influence of Machiavelli's teaching upon political action in successive generations after his death. I do not propose to deal with any of these matters, but to concentrate attention upon the narrower problem of the motive and purpose which induced Machiavelli to write one particular book, *Il Principe*. This problem, in comparison with the others to which most commentators have treated the book, in connection with the *Discorsi*, as a deliberate statement of Machiavelli's views as to the methods which should be adopted in founding, extending, and maintaining a principality. In this assumption they have been encouraged and confirmed by the author's inveterate habit of stating his propositions in the most general terms. . . .

In order to make my position clear it is necessary to offer some preliminary observations, which I will make as short as possible. *The Prince* was written in the later months of 1513, and Machiavelli's motives were necessarily conditioned by the contemporary state of affairs (1) in Europe, (2) in Italy generally, and in two Italian states with which he was peculiarly concerned, (3) the States of the Church, and (4) his own city of Florence.

(1) As to Europe, it is a commonplace

From Sir Richard Lodge, "Machiavelli's *Il Principe*," *Transactions of the Royal Historical Society*, 4th Series, Vol. XIII (1930), pp. 1–16. By permission of the Royal Historical Society.

to state that the mediaeval conception of the Holy Roman Empire was for all practical purposes obsolete at the close of the fifteenth century. Beyond the ever narrowing bounds of what was still called the Empire, states were forming themselves under the influence of that novel and undefinable force which we call nationality. England was politically outside the Florentine's ken, but two of the newly coherent states, France and Spain, were vitally concerned with the problems which troubled him. In both these states such unity as had been achieved was associated with a dynasty, with the increased authority of the crown, and with the overthrow of aristocratic privileges and independence. If you wish to realise how strongly this process of unification impressed Machiavelli, you have only to read what he says of the part played by the Parliament of Paris in bringing about the unity of France.

(2) From the prevalent tendency towards a national grouping of states in western Europe, Italy seemed to be comparatively exempt. It is needless to examine into the causes of Italian disunion. A nominal subjection to an alien and distant monarchy in Germany, the quarrels of Empire and Papacy with the resultant factions of Ghibellines and Guelfs, the obstinate traditions of municipal republicanism, all combined with the influence of geography to break up northern and central Italy into a number of minute political units. Such unifying influences as found their way into the peninsula took the form of the substitution of despotisms for democratic or oligarchical institutions, and of the subjection of the lesser states to their more powerful neighbours. By this process of local centralisation Italy came in the fifteenth century to be dominated by five principal states, the duchy of Milan, Venice, Florence, the Papacy, and the Kingdom of Naples. All progress towards more complete unification was checked by temporary coalitions against any state which threatened to overthrow the balance of power between these predominant units.

This uneasy and fluctuating balance could at any moment be destroyed by the calling in of a foreign power. For generations southern Italy had been involved in constant wars by the rival claims of the houses of Anjou and Aragon. At the end of the fifteenth century these claims passed to the ruling dynasties of France and Spain, and when Louis XII added to his Neapolitan claim a pretension to the duchy of Milan, the whole peninsula, north as well as south, was involved in this clash between the two major states of the continent. The German king, by virtue of his claim to imperial suzerainty in Italy, could not hold aloof from the contest, and thus Italy became the cockpit of Europe. In these incessant wars the Italian states themselves could only play an ignoble part, because the mercenary troops which they had employed for generations in their local feuds proved to be no match for the French or the Spaniards or even for the alien mercenaries who were brought in from Switzerland. Thus Italy seemed to lose not only all prospect of unity but almost all hope of independence. Such independence as was left to some of the states was only maintained by playing off one foreign invader against the other, a game which was both difficult and hazardous.

(3) The fifteenth century was a notable epoch in the history of the Papacy. The Latin Church, though more stable and more deeply-rooted than the Holy Roman Empire, appeared to be doomed to share its fate. A mortal blow to its claim to universality was dealt when the Council of Constance was divided into units whose ecclesiastical decisions were largely guided by political interests, thus justifying their academic name of "nations," and when Martin V foiled the schemes of the reforming party by concluding concordats with the separate states. From this it was but a step to the semi-political secessions of the following century. The process of disruption was hastened by the absorption of Martin V and his successors in the task of restoring papal control in the ecclesiastical

states, which had been torn to pieces by the great baronial houses during the Babylonish Captivity in Avignon and the Great Schism. After alternating success and failure on the part of intermediate Popes, the suppression of the nobles and princes in Rome and the Romagna was practically completed by Alexander VI and Caesar Borgia, whose policy Machiavelli had occasion to observe closely when he was sent on missions to Caesar's camp. Their aim, as he admits, was to found a secular principality for the house of Borgia, but the fruit of their achievements was reaped by the Papacy under Julius II. Julius was the real founder of the Papal States, and he thrust them into the seething cauldron of Italian politics. After humbling Venice by means of the League of Cambray, he turned against the French, raised the patriotic cry of "down with the foreigner," and organised the Holy League. He succeeded in his immediate aim, the eviction of the French from Lombardy, but he only did so by an inconsistent alliance with Spain, and thus helped to rivet upon Italy the chains of its first permanent subjection to foreign domination. On his death in 1513 the Papal States, with all the prominence which he had given to them, passed to his successor, Giovanni dei Medici, who took the name of Leo X.

(4) During the fifteenth century Florence had preserved her republican institutions, but the two great Medici, Cosimo, *Pater Patriae,* and his grandson, Lorenzo the Magnificent, had so manipulated them as to establish a personal rule which was none the less absolute because it was disguised. On Lorenzo's death in 1492, a fateful date for Italy and for Europe, this rule was assumed by his incompetent eldest son, Piero. Two years later Charles VIII's famous march through Italy resulted in the expulsion of Piero and his brothers, and Florence became once more a pure Republic. As its revival was due to France, the republican government remained, in spite of some vacillations, loyal to the French alliance during the prolonged wars

which followed. It was under this government that Machiavelli was employed and obtained his insight not only into domestic administration but also into the general currents of Italian and European politics. He was Secretary to the Council of Ten and was sent on several legations in Italy and twice to the Court of France. The period of republican revival was not a very triumphant one. Internal disorders, in which the rise and fall of Savonarola were involved, led to the adoption of an extreme remedy, the appointment of a Gonfalonier for life, in imitation of the Venetian Doge. Still more humiliating than domestic strife were the revolt of Pisa, the greatest conquest of the old Republic, and the disasters which accompanied the twelve years' siege that was required before the rebel city was reduced. And in the end the Republic had to pay dearly for its adhesion to France. In 1512, during the war of the Holy League, Spanish and Papal forces, under the guidance of the Cardinal dei Medici, occupied Florence, deposed the Republican Gonfalonier, and restored the constitution as before 1494, which meant the restoration of Medici rule. Machiavelli was deprived of his office and, after a short period of imprisonment for his services to the Republic, retired with his wife and family to his little estate near San Casciano, where he sought consolation for his impotence and poverty in the exercise of his pen. His favourite study was Roman history, and, taking Livy as his text, he began to write the *Discorsi* in which he commented upon the Roman historian in the light of his own political experience.

This then was the situation in 1513 as Machiavelli surveyed it. Italy was not only more torn and divided than ever but was under the heel of the foreigner: in his own words, "more enslaved than the Hebrews, more servile than the Persians, more dispersed than the Athenians, without a head, without order, beaten, despoiled, ravaged, over-run, and enduring every kind of ruin." It is true that one of the great invaders, France, had been for the moment driven from Italian soil, but it was not likely that its expulsion would be permanent. And in the meantime Spanish rule had been firmly fixed in southern Italy, and the imperial suzerainty, so long purely nominal, had been revived in the north by the return of the Sforzas to Milan. In his own city the Republic which had employed him had been overthrown, and the rule of the Medici had been restored under the protecting patronage of the now powerful Papal State. As long as Leo X was Pope, and he was still a comparatively young man, it was not humanly probable that the power of the ruling house, whether wielded by the Pope's brother, Giuliano, or by his nephew, the youthful Lorenzo, would be overthrown. Gradually there seems to have dawned upon Machiavelli's mind the idea that Italy's salvation might be found in this opportune conjunction of Florence with the Papacy. If only Leo would give to his brother or his nephew the support which Alexander VI had given to Caesar Borgia, and if he would adhere to the antiforeign programme put forward in his later years by Julius II, there might be built up a central Italian principality strong enough to extend its power to the Alps, and to establish there a barrier against any renewed invasion from France and against any active intervention on the part of Maximilian or his successors in Germany. It is hardly to be supposed that Machiavelli contemplated anything so chimerical as the expulsion of Spain from its southern kingdom. Naples had always been apart from Italy; its whole history was in complete contrast to that of the rest of the peninsula; it had not been included in that Lombard kingdom whose crown had been assumed by the mediaeval Emperors. The Italy which Machiavelli dreamed of as united and free was bounded on the south by the States of the Church.

Having dreamed his dream, Machiavelli was confronted with the problem of its realisation. It was obvious to him that neither pen nor voice could suffice. It would be useless to come out into the open, to denounce Italian degeneracy, to point out its causes, and to prescribe his heroic remedies, which included the formation of a national militia to supersede the fatal mercenaries of the past. He had watched the career of Savonarola, had contrasted it with that of past leaders from Moses downwards, and had come to his famous conclusion that it is only the armed prophets who have prevailed; the unarmed have always been ruined. He would not play the part of the unarmed prophet. Nor could he see any prospect of success in a revival, even if it had been possible, of republican independence. As he looked round Europe, he found that all the great achievements of his time were the work of princes. If the Medici prince, either Giuliano or Lorenzo, would undertake to serve the cause of Italy, it would be a small sacrifice on his own part to abandon any theoretical predilections for a Florentine Republic. Inspired by these conceptions, he turned aside from his *Discorsi* to write with great rapidity his manual of instructions for such member of the ruling family as would be willing to follow them. His first idea seems to have been to send his work to Giuliano, as the more amenable to advice and the more likely to conciliate support both in Florence and outside. But when Giuliano died in 1516, he had no alternative but to dedicate it to Lorenzo, and it is the Letter to Lorenzo which is prefixed to all editions of *The Prince*. There was of course no idea at the time of publication. Nothing could be more fatal to the purpose of the book than publicity. And as a matter of fact it was not printed until 1532, after Machiavelli's death, long after the death of Leo X, at a time when all hope of Italian unity had disappeared.

It is not in the least necessary to assume that Machiavelli believed in the possession by either of the Medici princes of the qualities which he desiderated. But a prince can be guided by a far-seeing and capable minister. As Machiavelli pointed out, it is in the choice of such a minister that the wisdom of the prince is demonstrated. I have never been able to read the brief twenty-second chapter on "the Secretaries of Princes" without a conviction that Machiavelli aspired to play to his prospective patron the part that Antonio da Venafro played to Pandolfo Petrucci of Siena. Nor do I see anything discreditable in the supposition, which I believe to be true, that a minor motive for writing *The Prince* was a desire on the part of the author to pave the way for his own return to political employment.

One last explanatory observation. I have said that Machiavelli turned from writing the *Discorsi* to compose *The Prince*. Any author can understand that he could not altogether free himself from the influence of his previous work. It was largely from this that he took those general assertions that sound so often as if he was laying down the law for all time, and it was wholly from this that he borrowed those classical illustrations and parallels which often seem out of place in a manual for a sixteenth-century ruler, and which rarely add much force to his contentions.

I admit that this reconstruction of Machiavelli's motives is largely conjectural, as indeed most interpretations of past motives must necessarily be. But I claim that it fits in with internal evidence, and it is not, so far as I know, contradicted by any external proof. Of course it may be incomplete: so subtle and complex a mind as that of Machiavelli may well have had other thoughts in reserve. But, so far as it goes, its refutation seems to me difficult and indeed impossible. And it has the supreme merit of removing most of the difficulties which have confronted commentators. It provides a complete answer to those doctrinaire republicans who have denounced Machiavelli as a traitor to his avowed principles because he wrote what appear to be maxims for despots. It explains and justifies the all-important chapter on Ecclesiastical Principalities, with its concluding compliment to Leo X, which appears to be quite irrelevant to the guidance of any normal secular ruler. Above all, it removes

what has been a stumbling-block to successive generations of critics, the choice of Caesar Borgia as an exemplar for Machiavelli's Prince. "I do not know," he says, "what better precepts I can give to a new prince than the example of his actions." This is a matter of such vital importance from my point of view that I may be allowed to develop it at some length.

Machiavelli divides new principalities into two categories according to whether they are acquired by *virtu* or by *fortuna*. *Virtu,* which may be regarded as the keyword of the Italian Renaissance, has nothing in common with our own word "virtue." It retains the classical meaning of courage or daring, but has acquired in addition the sense of intellectual ability. Fortune, on the other hand, is opportunity or environment. The man who can suit his conduct to contemporary conditions is called fortunate. If the conditions change and his conduct remains unaltered, he at once becomes unfortunate. If a man is skilful enough to change his conduct to suit changing circumstances — *temporeggiare con gli accidenti* — he will be always fortunate. The man who acquires a principality by *virtu* has all his difficulty in gaining his position, but little trouble in maintaining it; whereas the prince who rises by fortune, leaps suddenly to the summit, but requires all his skill and pains to keep himself there. Admitting Machiavelli's distinction, which of the two categories would be the more likely to fit an imaginary prince? There seems to me to be only one possible answer to the question. A prince who was worth advising might be expected to possess or develop *virtu*, or at least to choose a minister who would supply the desired quality. *Fortuna,* on the other hand, was a matter of luck and could not be had for the bidding. It was to be expected therefore that the preceptor of princes in general would lay stress upon the exercise and the reward of ability, and would pay comparatively little attention to careers which owed their starting-point to the chance of good fortune which was not likely to be repeated. But if we turn to *Il Principe* we find that Machiavelli does the precise opposite. He refers to Francesco Sforza as a prince who owed his elevation to *virtu,* and then dismisses him in a sentence. But to the career of Caesar Borgia, whom he selects as the beneficiary of fortune, he devotes a long and detailed chapter. This was not due, as is generally assumed, to his personal familiarity with the doings of the Borgias, or to any peculiar admiration for Caesar's character or achievements, but solely to the curious similarity of his *fortuna* with that of the restored Medici in Florence. Caesar Borgia was the son of a Pope. It could not be expected that any normal prince in the dim future would find himself so situated. But Giuliano dei Medici was the brother, and Lorenzo was the nephew, of the actually reigning Pope. This fact, and nothing else, made Caesar an apt example, not for all princes, but for the particular ruler to whom *Il Principe* was to be addressed.

This narrows the much-debated problem of political morality. Machiavelli himself leaves no doubt on this matter in his fifteenth chapter. He will say nothing about imaginary princes, but will confine himself to contemporary facts.

My intention being to write something that may be useful to him who understands, it has seemed to me more fitting to go behind to the actual truth about things rather than to any imaginary condition: and indeed there are many imagined republics and principalities which have never been known to exist in fact; for there is so great a distance between the way men live and the way they ought to live, that he who quits what is actually done for that which ought to be done, will bring about his ruin rather than his safety; because a man who wishes to be virtuous in all his actions must necessarily be ruined among so many who are not virtuous.

The general conclusion of the chapter is that a prince should, if possible, possess all the virtues, but that in a wicked world he must exercise such self-control that, while avoiding all vices which might ruin the state, he should not be too scrupulous about those which are necessary for its salvation. This is no general maxim for all time: it is advice to an Italian prince in the early part of the sixteenth century. The "wicked world" is the world as Machiavelli saw it. And I confess that, startling or even shocking as it may sound to us at the present day, I do not see what other advice he could have given. If Machiavelli's premises are accepted, it is difficult to resist his conclusions. His most voluminous critic does not defend the political morality of Italy, but contends at great length that things were just as bad in England, France, and Spain in the same age. This may be consoling to Italians, but it does not affect the contention that a political writer, like a political actor, must be judged by the prevalent morals of his own time rather than by any absolute code. I once had occasion to read an interesting correspondence on this subject between Lord Acton and Bishop Creighton. The layman was for the moral code, the whole code, and nothing but the code, while the Bishop pleaded for some allowance for the historic wrong-doer. I own that in this controversy I am on the side of the Bishop. And I must reiterate my conviction that Machiavelli was writing not only about his own time but for his own time and for no other.

This last paragraph is a partial digression into one of those topics which I had determined to avoid. But it is difficult, in writing about Machiavelli, to avoid such a digression. I have still my final argument in the famous last chapter in which he urges the recipient of his book to undertake the sublime task of freeing Italy from the barbarians. I have already quoted from it his picture of the forlorn condition of his native country, and I cannot refrain from one last extract, though no translation can do justice to what is perhaps the finest example of Italian prose.

There is no visible hope for Italy except in your illustrious house, if, with its *virtu* and its *fortuna* [I lay stress upon this last word], favoured by God and the Church, of which it is now the head [I lay stress again on these words], it will take the lead in the country's redemption. . . . No words can express with what joy it will be received in all those provinces which have suffered from these foreign floods, with what thirst for vengeance, with what resolute faith, with what devotion, with what tears. What gates will be closed to the redeemer? What people will refuse him obedience? What jealousy will oppose him? What Italian will deny him devotion? In every man's nostrils this barbarous dominion stinks. Let therefore your illustrious house undertake this venture with the courage and the hope with which men embark on just enterprises in order that under its standard this country may be ennobled, and under its auspices this sonnet of Petrarch may be verified:

"Virtu contro al furore
Prendera l'arme, e fia il combatter corto;
Chè l'antico valore
Negl' Italici cuor non è ancor morto."[1]

I have never been able to understand, much less to sympathise with, the contention advanced in some quarters, that this chapter was mere rhetorical camouflage to conceal and justify the deliberate immorality of the rest of the book. If Machiavelli was not sincere when he wrote this, I should lose all faith in the sincerity of any writer. And a man does not write deliberate camouflage to blind the eyes of posterity when he does not know that what he writes will ever meet those eyes.

I can imagine a destructive critic maintaining that the *Principe,* as I have interpreted it, reveals a scheme so chimerical in itself, and proved to be so chimerical by subsequent events, that it can never have been seriously put forward by a man with such an acute intellect and so much practical experience as Machiavelli possessed. I do not accept the conclusion. Machiavelli

[1] I have not ventured to translate the lines of Petrarch, but Madame Villari has, quite justifiably, been bolder. Her rendering is:

"When Virtue takes arms against Fury, short will be the fight,
For in Italian hearts still lives the ancient might."

very probably underestimated certain difficulties, but, even if he had been less sanguine, he would not be the first advocate of a great cause who believed that it would be more advanced by unsuccessful effort than by passive acquiescence. But I admit that the project was chimerical. Its weakest point was the belief that the Papacy would combine with Florence for its promotion. This is probably clearer to us than it was to Machiavelli. For a century before 1513 the Popes had weakened and almost sacrificed their claim to the spiritual headship of a universal Church while they concentrated their efforts on the building up of a temporal lordship. Machiavelli himself had seen Alexander VI lending the papal name and papal support to the unscrupulous schemes of Caesar Borgia. And he had seen Julius II acting as a secular prince, leading troops to the war, and proclaiming a sort of Italian crusade against the French. It was not altogether surprising that he left out of account the spiritual side of the Papacy, and believed that the policy of Leo X would be as frankly secular as that of his recent predecessors. But he reckoned without the Reformation. The Lutheran movement with its threat of schism, the actual secession of England, of the north German princes, and the Scandinavian countries, forced the Popes to revive their old claims, to refurbish their ancient weapons, and in the end to consent to a reform of the old Church. It then became clear that the Papacy was by its very nature pledged to war against the principle of nationality, and especially against nationality in the country in which the Popes lived. One of the first acts of the reformed Papacy was to place the works of Machiavelli upon the Index. When in the nineteenth century Italian unity and independence were at last achieved, the Papacy held obstinately aloof and hostile, and it has been left to our own day to witness the signature of a possibly fragile treaty between the head of the Roman Church and the King of a united Italy. In spite of the treaty, the relations between the Vatican and the Quirinal are likely to be uneasy for some time to come.

While Machiavelli was blind as to the spiritual revival of the Papacy, and its consequent desertion of the cause of Italy, which Julius II had seemed for the moment to have espoused, there was another untoward event which he could not foresee. This was the union under Charles V of the Spanish monarchy with the Austrian inheritance and the Imperial pretensions. The overwhelming power wielded by Charles V was responsible for the establishment of that Spanish domination in Italy, which was transmitted from the Spanish to the Austrian Habsburgs, which was restored in 1815 after the shattering blows of Napoleon, and was not finally overthrown till the middle of last century. And even then it was not overthrown by unaided Italian effort, but by the classic expedient of playing off one foreign state against another.

Although Machiavelli's dream was unrealised, though no Medici aspired to play the part of Victor Emmanuel, or called upon him to play the part of Cavour, and though Italy was ultimately freed by other methods than those which he had devised, his whole-hearted advocacy of his country's cause has never been forgotten, and ever since the middle of the last century he has stood higher in the estimation of his fellow-countrymen than at any other time since his death.

The Nationalism of Machiavelli

FELIX GILBERT

There is little doubt that Felix Gilbert, professor of history at Bryn Mawr College and a member of the executive board of the Renaissance Society of America, is one of the most active American scholars in the field of Machiavelli studies. After several years abroad, where he received his Ph.D. in 1931 at Berlin, Gilbert returned to the Institute of Advanced Study at Princeton, and then served with the O.S.S. and the U.S. State Department from 1943 to 1946. In the autumn of 1959 he was a visiting professor of modern history at the University of Cologne. Gilbert is well known not only for his many articles and contributions to Renaissance topics, but also for his perceptive scholarship in the fields of diplomatic and military history. He is a contributor to and co-editor of *The Diplomats, 1919–1939,* and editor of *Hitler Directs His War.*

OF all the writings of Machiavelli, none has been so much commented upon as *The Prince,* and of the various sections of *The Prince,* none has been discussed so much as the last chapter. The chapter is an "exhortation to liberate Italy from the Barbarians." Machiavelli believes that the opportunity has come "to introduce a new system" in Italy. A new Prince should place himself at the head of the Italians, who are "ready and willing to follow any standard, if only there be someone to raise it."

What doors would be closed against him? What people would refuse him obedience? What enemy could oppose him? What Italian would withhold allegiance? This barbarous domination stinks in the nostrils of every one.

Machiavelli feels sure that the Barbarians could not withstand the impact of the Italian forces united under a new Prince. "This opportunity must not, therefore, be allowed to pass, so that Italy may at length find her liberator."

There are two reasons for the great attention which this chapter has aroused. The dramatic appeal to nationalism seems most strange in a stage of political development where nationalism, if it plays any role at all, has certainly not an important part. And it is particularly astonishing to find this reliance on popular enthusiasm in Machiavelli; there is a striking difference between the emotional idealism which pervades the national appeal of the last chapter of *The Prince* and the cold and realistic analysis of political forces which forms the distinguishing feature of the rest of the work.

Although the full extent of the problem involved in Machiavelli's appeal to nationalism has been appreciated only in more recent studies, the difference between the last chapter and the rest of the book has been noticed ever since critical scholarship began to occupy itself with the work. Ranke, in his first historical work, was struck by this contrast and wrote: "Let us be just! He sought the salvation of Italy, but her situation seemed to him so desperate that he was bold enough to prescribe poison." Thus Ranke saw in Machiavelli

From Felix Gilbert, "The Concept of Nationalism in Machiavelli's *Prince*," *Studies in the Renaissance,* I (1954), pp. 38–48. Reprinted by permission of the author and The Renaissance Society of America.

primarily an Italian patriot, and his sentences set the tone for the discussion of the problem throughout the nineteenth century. Machiavelli's realism seemed justified as it aimed at the fulfillment of national aspirations; Machiavelli was seen as the prophet of the modern national state. This conception of Machiavelli could seem plausible to the historians of the nineteenth century because they were inclined to see history, especially from the Renaissance on, as developing in a straight line toward the modern world.

However, Ranke's explanation of Machiavelli's emphasis on nationalism appeared questionable to the historians of the twentieth century, whose concepts of history have taken on a more relativistic tinge and who are more skeptical about considering the past mainly as the seedbed of the present. It was observed that Machiavelli's ideas regarding the union of Italy in the last chapter of *The Prince* remained vague. It is not clear whether he envisaged a transitory military alliance, a permanent federal constitution, or a unified national state. It was also noticed that on other occasions he expressed much less confidence in the enthusiasm of the Italians to fight for the freedom of their country. Thus the question was asked whether the Italian nationalism advocated in the last chapter of *The Prince* could really be regarded as a central issue in Machiavelli's political thought or whether this chapter ought not to be considered as a purely rhetorical ending, a humanist peroration. This was the problem which Meinecke raised thirty years ago in his edition of *The Prince*.

In order to determine the significance of the last chapter within the work as a whole, Meinecke embarked on an investigation of the process of its composition. He attempted to show that *The Prince* was not the result of a single brilliant inspiration, but that different layers could be distinguished, indicating that the work was composed in sections. Meinecke's thesis was vehemently disputed by Federico Chabod, who insisted that *The Prince* was written by Machia-

velli during 1513, in a very brief span of time; he concluded, therefore, that the work must have originated out of a unified conception. This was the beginning of a controversy between "divisionists" and "unifiers." Chabod and his adherents directed attention to the manner in which fundamental concepts of the last chapter — like the motif of the state founders — have been foreshadowed in previous sections of *The Prince,* so that the appeal to nationalism really forms the conscious climax of the work, while advocates of the opposite point of view can refer to the discovery of literary models of the work or point to investigations of the language showing the particularly Petrarchesque style of the last chapter.

As much as the adherents of the two differing points of view may feel sure of the correctness of their interpretation of the composition of *The Prince,* it seems to those less directly involved that agreement about the significance of the last chapter of *The Prince* has not been reached, that the decisive point has not yet been made.

The controversy certainly has not been fruitless, however, for it has had the unquestionable merit of increasing and refining our understanding of the character of the work. On the other hand, the problem of the role of nationalism in Machiavelli's thought has become entirely dependent on the problem of the composition of *The Prince* and has been absorbed by it. Actually, however, the question of whether the ideas of this chapter form an integral part of Machiavelli's thinking or are a purely rhetorical peroration is not exclusively dependent on whether the last chapter was a later addition or not. It would seem to be equally significant whether the ideas contained in this chapter are conventional or whether they express new and original thoughts, thereby indicating a serious concern with the problem of nationalism on Machiavelli's part. The intention of this paper is to direct attention to the possibilities of an approach which places the nationalistic appeal of the last chapter of *The*

Prince in relation to other expressions of nationalism in this period, and to make some tentative explorations along this line.

Federico Chabod has called this chapter a unique page in the literature of the Italian Renaissance. This statement clearly needs elucidation and interpretation, for it must be clear to every student of the Italian Renaissance that this uniqueness does not include the entire complex of ideas contained in the last chapter of *The Prince*, but only certain of its aspects.

There is certainly nothing new in the fundamental presupposition — in the idea of Italy as a unit distinguished from the surrounding world, in the demand for the expulsion of the foreigners. Machiavelli himself concludes the chapter with a quotation from Petrarch's *Italia Mia* which had already expressed these ideas; and in the fourteenth century the sentiment of Petrarch's *Canzone* had been re-echoed in the works of other poets, by Fazio Degli Uberti, Francesco di Vanozzo, and the poets of the Visconti court. It was natural to fall back on this tradition when a situation similar to that from which Petrarch's song originated had arisen.

In the fifteenth century — in the period of relaxation of outside pressure and of a relative autonomy of Italian political life — the praise of the individual city or state which the humanists served, the defense of its eminence over all others, became favorite themes of humanist political writings. But even in this narrower framework, the humanists did not lose sight of the larger unity within which the single state existed. Salutati praised Florence because in defending her own freedom she had "saved liberty in Italy." The intellectual primacy which humanism had given to Italy even intensified the feeling of the separateness of Italy from the rest of Europe. It is a recurrent theme in humanist literature that Italy has a special position in the world because her frontiers were drawn by nature herself. The view that Italy was a separate geographical unit on whose soil foreign Barbarians have no right to be, is a fundamental assumption of humanist political reflections.

Difficult as it is to gauge whether and how far these views reached beyond the group of the humanistically educated, there is enough evidence to show that the renewal of an era of foreign invasions which opened with the expedition of Charles VIII resulted in the awakening of a national feeling in wider groups. We have popular songs directed against the foreigners; we know that in 1509, before the battle of Agnadello, the soldiers shouted "Italy, Italy," into the face of their foreign opponents. A technician like Birigucci suddenly inserts in his book on pyrotechnics a passionate appeal for a war of revenge and a demand for the return of the treasures which the foreign nations had looted from Italy. But the clearest proof of the extent to which thinking in national terms had become general can be found in Florentine diaries, not only of the ruling group, but also of the middle classes. Of course, outbreaks of resentment against particular cruelties and atrocities of the foreign soldiers are only natural at all times in such situations and do not deserve particular attention. It is significant, however, how in those complaints about the "destruction" of the country, about the "slavery" into which it had fallen, Italy comes alive — it appears as the poor, mistreated woman of the earlier songs. It can be observed also that a feeling of the common fate of the Italians has entered the political consciousness. It is reflected in the irreconcilable hatred with which Lodovico Moro is regarded as responsible for the misfortunes of Italy and in the tense excitement with which the news of the outcome of the conclave after the death of Alexander VI is expected — whether the election would fall on a foreigner or an Italian. "Italy should be ruled by Italians and not by Oltramontani," writes Vaglienti.

These are no new insights, but these facts deserve to be mentioned in this context, because they help to define more clearly the characteristic features of Machiavelli's chapter. The chapter reflects elements in the climate of opinion of the time. The distinguishing fact is that Machiavelli fuses these elements together into a program of political action. The evaluation of the uniqueness of Machiavelli's chapter depends, therefore, on the importance of the national idea in political action, on its connection with the political practice of its time. In more concrete form: what is the relation of Machiavelli's ideas to the various attempts to form an Italian league against the foreigners? In the years preceding the writing of *The Prince* the chief efforts of this kind were made against Charles VIII, first before his coming and then after the conquest of Naples, then against the designs of Louis XII on Milan and then by Julius II. Even in the most recent literature the leading powers in these attempts — in particular Venice and Julius II — have been regarded as being inspired by a serious concern for the national independence of Italy.

Certainly the appeal to national interest is strong in all these negotiations. Immediately at the reopening of the era of foreign invasions, these considerations are movingly and eloquently expressed in the instructions which Pontano, as Chancellor of the Neapolitan King, composed in order to deflect the Borgia Pope and Lodovico Moro from their pro-French course. He drew a sharp line between the particular interest of each power and the common interest. Considering the geographical situation of Italy, a dissension among its powers could only lead to oppression by the Oltramontani, who, as they had in the past, would again become Italy's tyrants. Sometime later when French troops were entering on Italian soil, a desperate attempt was made by the Pope and Florence to induce Venice to join the coalition against Charles VIII. The language in which these negotiations were couched was again that of the common national interest: they criticized the Venetians for wanting "to stay securely in port and to see the other powers weaken and suffer"; it was necessary to be "a good

Italian," to have regard for the "universal danger" and "universal needs of Italy."

It is almost ironical to see how Lodovico Moro, Charles VIII's former ally, takes recourse to almost identical appeals when a few years later his rule is threatened by Charles' successor, and when he wants the Florentines to support him and to abandon the French connection. Lodovico is not unaware, however, of the weakness of his position as a defender of common national interests against the foreigners. It is striking — and perhaps indicative of an increased sensitivity — that he considers it necessary frequently to apologize for his role in 1494. In contrast he stresses the part he played in forging the Italian coalition, which forced Charles' retreat from Naples. But, if nothing else, Lodovico's discussions with the Florentine ambassadors show to what extent expressions like "the common well-being of Italy," and the "liberty and independence of Italy" were the common currency of the diplomatic vocabulary. But these negotiations reveal also the limits of the meaning of these terms. Lodovico warns the Florentines against the Venetians, who through their alliance with France want to become rulers over Italy. The warning against the foreigners is always connected with the fear that as a result of the upheaval of a foreign invasion a foreign or even an Italian power might attain hegemony over Italy. Independence and liberty of Italy has the double meaning of keeping the Oltramontani away, but also of preserving individual Italian powers in their independence, of maintaining the status quo.

This interconnection of Italian independence with the sovereignty of the individual state necessarily raises the question whether this national terminology is anything but ideology. The national interest could easily be appealed to — as it was by Naples, by Venice, by Lodovico Moro, by Julius II — when their own existence was threatened. But did it possess any reality beyond that of a pleasant and generally acceptable disguise of the pursuit of a purely egotistical policy by the individual Italian state?

An incident which pierces through the clouds of conventional terminology into concrete motivations occurred in the decisive weeks of the fall of 1494, when French troops began to enter northern Italy. The Florentine and Papal ambassadors had increased their efforts to reach an understanding with Venice. In a dramatic conversation the Papal legate said that the Doge would acquire eternal fame if, in the present situation of danger for Italy, he would participate in the attempt to liberate her, to secure her against the infidels and to maintain her in her independence. Faced by this passionate appeal, the Doge seems to have felt that conventional assurances that Venice had the interest and the well-being of Italy at heart would not suffice. "You are considered a man of good will," he said to the Papal legate; "tell me the truth upon your own conscience: Would you seriously advise us to take sides against such a powerful ruler as the King of France and against his ally Lodovico of Milan . . . and consequently submit to a war and its calamities which would certainly bring endless disorder and might mean ruining our state and all we have?"

We also have the protocols of the meetings in which the leading Florentine citizens discussed, at the end of the century and the time of Julius II, what answer ought to be given to the demands of the popes to join the league against France. In these discussions, almost all the speakers agree about the language to be used. It ought to be emphasized that the Florentines have always been "good Italians," and intended to remain so. They feel themselves different from the barbarian people beyond the Alps. In their practical considerations, however, the speakers are concerned only with Florence; in general they prefer neutrality; they consider the influence which a change of front would have on Florentine chances to reconquer Pisa; they regard the maintenance of the French alliance a necessity because of the Florentine economic interests in France. Other than immediately practical considerations do not enter the discussions. Another example, though it comes from a later period, namely from the time after the battle of Pavia, may have some special interest because the paper was written when, with the overpowering strength of Charles V, the danger of a complete loss of Italian independence had become much closer and because the author is Machiavelli's great friend, Francesco Vettori. It is the time of the beginnings of the negotiations which led to the League of Cognac; the Pope had asked Vettori's advice whether to embark on this course. Vettori had no doubt that Charles aspired at hegemony over Italy, and for this reason he would consider it to be the duty of the Italian powers and in particular of the Pope to act against this plan, but there is one condition — such glorious enterprise, writes Vettori, could be recommended only if it could be done in safety. If the Emperor would really attempt to extinguish the existence of the Papal state, then one might have to adopt the policy which would risk everything in the common cause; but when one might be able to remain alive, there is no reason for embarking on a course which might be suicidal. This document is a typical reflection of that tone of rational calculation with which the Florentines of this period approach the practical discussions of foreign policy.

These observations would indicate that national considerations do not enter the deliberations about the course to be followed in foreign policy. The standard formulas which humanism had created, the rise of a national sentiment, the diplomatic tradition of the Italian Leagues, are all on a different level from that on which the diplomatic negotiations were actually conducted. But it would not be right to confine oneself to this entirely negative conclusion. For the strange fact is that the same men who seem little influenced by national considerations in their political practice, who, in the Pratiche, discuss foreign policy alone from the point of view of Florentine local interest, remain fascinated by the problem in their reflections. Because when the Rucellai, the Vettori, the Guicciardini write about the fifteenth century as the lost paradise, as a period in which Italian independence was maintained because peace was preserved through the successful operation of a system of an Italian balance of power, what else are they doing but drawing from the fact of the victory of the foreigners the conclusion that a national policy, a policy of cooperation among the Italian powers, could have been successful and that Italy was ruined by placing the interest of the individual state over the common interest? The transference of the issue into the past may disguise the problem, but it cannot be denied that it is the concern with the national issue which takes here the indirect form of a historical reconstruction.

Evidently, there is an inevitability in the inclusion of this problem in the political discussions. Thus the particular features of Machiavelli's approach are of a rather limited character. It is neither concern with this question in general nor the attempt to direct practical politics toward the maintenance of Italian liberty and independence which distinguishes his appeal, but the recommendation of carrying out this policy over the head of the individual state, relying on the feeling of the masses. In all other cases, such plans were conceived in the framework of cooperation of the individual states. This points to the fact that there is still another dimension within which the problem of Italian nationalism in the Renaissance has to be placed: namely its relation to internal policy, the limitation of the practical concern with the national issue by domestic policy. The aristocrats who ruled Florence neither could nor would advance — practically or theoretically — to a position which would destroy the basis of their rule; in their eyes the interconnection between the independence of Italy and the independence of the indi-

vidual state was an absolute necessity. Machiavelli was not an aristocrat either personally or politically. On the contrary, his theories were directed against the rational political approach of the Florentine ruling group. The protocols of the Pratiche make this very clear: the participants of these meetings were almost exclusively members of the Florentine ruling group, and the protocols of these discussions can be considered as the most authentic and most uncensored expression of their views. In his function as secretary Machiavelli was present at many of these meetings and it is significant, therefore, that many of the views which he expresses in *The Prince* and in *The Discourses* are contradictions of individual views of speakers in the Pratiche as well as of the general presuppositions of their political approach. Also, in his attitude to the national issue, Machiavelli would necessarily take a different line.

It is evident that in so far as Machiavelli possessed contact with a political party, it was with the opponents of the Florentine ruling group, the so-called democrats. Adherents of the republic and the Great Council, they were kept out of government by the Medici; but, drawing their inspiration from the political and religious teachings of Savonarola, they remained a distinguishable opposition group in the times of the first Medici restoration, till, after a short period of rule, they were defeated and annihilated in 1530. Machiavelli was close to them not only because he shared their views for the need of a broad popular basis of government. The unifying bond among this opposition group was (as recent research has emphasized) a strong reform impulse, and something of the feeling of the necessity of an ethical Renaissance is underlying also Machiavelli's thinking. But with Machiavelli this reform impulse lacked the religious element while among the Florentine democrats the desired reform was seen chiefly in Christian and Church terms. This is a reason why, in this group, Machiavelli could not find any pattern for the formulation of the national issue either.

In its thinking on foreign policy, this group would remain restricted to a local level or be led into universal perspectives because its outlook on foreign policy was determined by Savonarola's concept of Florence as the city of God and the demand for a renewal of the papacy in its universal function.

It is not possible to identify Machiavelli with any of the existing Florentine political parties; he had a position outside the party systems. Although his thinking emerged from the issues and problems raised in the conflicts of the Florentine parties, he transcended them through his novel approach; he was a revolutionary in his thinking. But this means that Machiavelli's thinking falls into the pattern which the revolutionary thinking of all times has taken. It is characteristic of revolutionary thinking that it emerges from the concrete problems of domestic policy and sees foreign policy in terms of a changed revolutionary world; its thoughts on foreign policy remain vague and utopian. Of that Machiavelli's handling of the national issue is an example, and this fact may help to explain the suggestive, puzzling, and elusive character of the last chapter of *The Prince*.

A PRODUCT AND SPOKESMAN OF RENAISSANCE ITALY

The Renaissance Prince

LAURENCE ARTHUR BURD

For many years the standard edition of *The Prince* was the 1891 Italian edition, with annotations and introduction by L. A. Burd, and with a general preface by Lord Acton. Burd's carefully prepared work was a highlight of editorial scholarship for its time. He also wrote a rather detailed study of the literary sources of Machiavelli's *Art of War*, published in Rome in 1897 as *Le fonti letterarie de Machiavelli nell'Arte della Guerra,* and contributed a chapter on Machiavelli in Volume II of *The Cambridge Modern History.*

To understand *The Prince* aright, it is not only necessary to go back to Machiavelli's age; the book must also be restored to Machiavelli's country. *The Prince* was never meant except for Italians, and Italians too of a given period; indeed, we may go further, and ask whether it was ever intended even for all Italians; it certainly bears the stamp of what a modern writer might call an esoteric treatise. But however that may be, the book was very soon taken outside Italy, and became the handbook of princes of many nations, familiar throughout the whole of Europe. It was translated into all the more important European languages, and the translations gave but little help toward appreciating the original; for, apart from the difficulty of so representing Machiavelli's words in a foreign language as to create the same impression as the original, some were translations of translations, and thus at least three times removed from the truth.

While *The Prince* enjoyed the popularity of all books which appear to offer a logical demonstration that dishonesty is the best policy, little attention was given to the circumstances under which it was composed, and ultimately the historical point of view was altogether lost. As its recovery seemed hopeless, those who felt that their moral sense had been outraged turned to the task, so easy and valueless, of abusing a writer whose writings they neglected. Even where attempts were made to frame an impartial estimate, little effort was made to discriminate between those parts of Machiavelli's writings which were meant to have a general application, *"semper ubique et ab omnibus,"* and those other portions which were determined by special and for the most part unusual and anomalous conditions. This inability to distinguish between the general and the particular portions, and the tendency to regard as universal maxims of political science what were only suggested as methods unfortunately rendered imperative in a given case, increased the difficulties of criticism tenfold. Portions of Machiavelli's doctrines were determined by the bent of his own mind, but a large part also by his age and country: under different circumstances many elements of his thought would have been different; and

From Laurence Arthur Burd (ed.), Introduction to Machiavelli's *Il Principe,* (Oxford: The Clarendon Press, 1891), pp. 14–17, 22–28. Reprinted by permission of the publishers.

criticism has often lost sight of this truism.

There are other difficulties which are in a measure inseparable from the form of expression which Machiavelli chose to adopt, and which, for the rest, was in fairly common use in his age. His style is epigrammatic, and lends itself to quotation: single sentences can be easily remembered, and yet are scarcely ever, when detached from their setting, an adequate measure of his thought: the "Mente di un uomo di stato" hardly gives a fairer idea of the writer than the strange "olla podrida" of mangled quotations which forms the staple commodity in the writings of Machiavelli's older opponents. And *The Prince,* and in a less degree all the other published writings of Machiavelli, excluding perhaps the *Legations,* are full of absolutely unqualified statements; Machiavelli did not feel so strongly as modern writers the difficulties of political science and the dangers of dogmatism, and hence has been at no pains to restrict his statements by any subordinate considerations which perhaps might have been necessary, but which would in any case have obscured the immediate issues. . . .

Machiavelli in *The Prince* has eliminated sentiment and morality, though the interest to him was not merely scientific, but practical also: he did so partly deliberately, and partly without any distinct consciousness that he was mutilating human nature. But whatever considerations determined the method he employed, he followed it without swerving, consistently and logically. Thus Cesare Borgia is viewed by him solely as a politician, and no word is allowed to the moralist. Whether by thus considering only one aspect of human nature at a time, he has vitiated his own conclusions, or whether this is rather the condition upon which alone he could solve the problem which he set himself, may be doubted; but it would be unfair in any case to argue from his silence and his omissions that he had lost the consciousness that man might be regarded as a moral being: he merely declined to allow moral considerations to interfere, as he believed they did,

with the logical discussion of the subject in hand. It was not his purpose to press further, and ask whether a political morality might not after all exist, differing perhaps from the morality of the individual in society in its greater complexity, and the larger number of cases of conscience which it presents for solution, but none the less binding because a simple necessity, a "sine qua non" for the existence of the state.

Machiavelli, then, while writing *The Prince,* kept before him one object alone, and deliberately selected to disregard everything else, neither asking what was the relation of his doctrines to other departments of enquiry, nor what their effect would be upon the life of society or of the individual. But each of the critics who came after him immediately raised the question, What will the application of such theories *do* to human life? and more specifically, What will they do to my own life? In other words, they suggested considerations, which it was not part of Machiavelli's business to enquire into, and in order to argue against him, they were forced to begin by missing his point. Finding that he did not regard men from the point of view of the moral philosopher, they concluded that his silence was equivalent to the denial by implication of the value of moral action altogether. Hence they remained for a long time mere controversialists, and lost sight of the legitimate objects of criticism in the desire to refute an antagonist. And an examination of the causes which produced the misunderstanding shows that it was in large part due to the form in which Machiavelli wrote: had he qualified his statements or been less consistently clear and distinct, he could hardly have been regarded as a monster of iniquity, or the master of those who do *not* know. . . .

The question still confronts us in its original form: What determined the composition of *The Prince?* In the last resort, only one answer can be given: The general condition of Italy. This answer is, at first sight, perhaps inadequate; but it is nevertheless the only one that is really satisfactory. We know that the ideas contained in *The Prince* took form in Machiavelli's mind very slowly; their importance forced itself upon him step by step; certainly he could not have reached them at a single bound. What must have struck Machiavelli, and any thoughtful Italian, as he followed in broad outline the history of his country, would be some such considerations as the following: he might not perhaps be fully conscious of them, but their influence, if only half-realised and ill-defined, would tend to create a feeling that the ordinary methods of government in use in the past, now needed revision and possibly radical alteration.

For more than a century before Machiavelli wrote, a continual process of disintegration had been going on in Central Italy and Lombardy. Within this area, whatever may have been the case in other parts of the peninsula, the centrifugal tendency had been almost exclusively operative, and had led to the formation of a large number of independent states with apparently incompatible interests. Without stopping to enquire how it was that at the very moment when France and Spain were being consolidated, and welded into compact homogeneous masses, Italy was becoming more and more incapable of united action, we may notice some of the more obvious results of this disunion. . . .

These perpetual changes led to two clearly defined results; first, the importance of the individual was exaggerated. When a government was revolutionised, the change was ascribed to the influence or ability or force of one man; and it is true that in many cases the individual was indeed the impelling force of a revolution. Individual ambition and class discontent were in a large degree the cause of the instability of power in Italy. But it is none the less true that the influence of the individual in shaping the general history of his country was largely overrated at the time. Machiavelli in this respect shared the belief of his age; he explained history as the creation of the individual, and when, in

The Prince, he called upon one man to free Italy from the "barbarians," so far from having any consciousness that the scheme would be chimerical, he rather believed that it had its full justification in experience and reason.

The second result was, that the notion of right was lost. The Emperor was more a name than a reality among the Italians of the Renaissance; and whilst the Popes were discrediting the institution they represented by their own immorality and ambition, the religious sense was decaying, and morality together with it was lost. The full, vigorous, and restless life, which fermented within the narrow bounds of each state, was exhausting the country; the perpetual necessity of watching themselves or their neighbours produced among the political rings that governed Italy a sense of mutual distrust; they were very zealous for their parochial fatherland: they were prepared to go to all lengths in its defence; but they dared not arm their own citizens, who might be made the instrument of conspiracy.

Under these circumstances it was natural that political success should depend mainly upon the exercise of superior shrewdness. Each "prince," whose power had no foundation in authority, was forced to rely upon himself, his own ready resource and acuteness; the exigencies of his position blinded him, more or less in different cases, to the character of the means he employed, provided only that the end was gained. "Tout ce que la politique commande, la justice l'autorise" was a maxim put into practice long before it was formulated; and though for a long time there was no conscious separation of the spheres of politics and common life, nor any formal determination of the duties of the politician *vis-à-vis* the individual in society, yet the moral aspect of every state question came to be dropped by a tacit understanding, till, as Machiavelli says, "della fede non si tiene oggi conto."

The Italians were not ignorant of the evils which were caused by their own disunion, but the majority felt strongly the hopelessness of any attempt to cope with them. Guicciardini, a thoroughly practical man, whose writings form the best comment upon Machiavelli, regarded any scheme for the unification of Italy as the idle vision of a dream; indeed he was almost inclined to think it undesirable in itself, and to regard the stimulating influence of a number of independent states as a compensation for the weakness of a divided nation. In any case he was convinced that Italy could not cut herself adrift from the past and, making a "tabula rasa" of her old institutions, take a fresh start at a given moment; and hence he rejected the idea of a great and general fatherland for all Italians, the notion of which had been gradually permeating the intellectual atmosphere. . . .

The character of the man upon whom the work of reformation is to devolve is sketched by Machiavelli in *The Prince*. He must in the first place be entirely free from emotional disturbance; he must be ready to take advantage of the existing state of things; he must be strong enough to sin boldly, if his country's welfare depends upon it; he must be shrewd enough to understand human nature in whatever form he finds it, and, overcoming evil by evil, play with the passions and impulses of men, use them as he pleases, force them to his purpose, manage them. And above all he must be thorough: a single hesitation, a single half-measure might compromise the whole result. He must depend upon himself and his own soldiers; he must abolish all mercenaries, and establish a national army of his own subjects. If such a man could be found, of unflinching purpose, dead to every sentiment but the love of his country, willing to save his fatherland rather than his own soul, careless of justice or injustice, of mercy or cruelty, of honour or disgrace, he might perhaps free Italy from foreign intervention, and begin the regeneration of his people. . . .

But as few books are ever written with one motive only, so in this case we can trace the influence of other subordinate considerations which determined the composition. There is much in *The Prince* that is without doubt intended as a contribution toward a new science of State, though Machiavelli has never been at pains to separate such portions from those more immediately determined by the complex conditions of contemporary Italian politics. Certainly the book contains much that is not merely intended for a new Prince; slight discussions of hereditary monarchies, of the Papacy, and of other forms of absolute government, give it somewhat the appearance of a general treatise, though the "principe armato," the armed reformer, is hardly ever lost sight of, and all the other branches of the discussion have a secondary importance and are hastily despatched.

Finally, we may be certain that the personal motive got inextricably mixed up with the others, affecting now the form of a sentence, and now the presentation of a thought, so that no one could fairly attempt to define today the exact influence which it had upon Machiavelli when he put pen to paper.

The most cursory examination of *The Prince* shows that the rules which Machiavelli has laid down for the guidance of a "new prince" run counter to all commonly accepted canons of morality; and if regarded as general maxims of politics they are hopelessly fallacious and inadequate. They were not meant as such, though they were often applied in cases widely dissimilar from that which Machiavelli had under examination. The "welthistorisch" importance of the book is due largely to its having been misunderstood. The details of *The Prince* can be easily refuted, but such a refutation is as valueless as easy. Much of its substance remains true always; and it has an importance of its own as a contribution to historical method, and as evidence of Italian feeling and of a gifted Italian's mind at a great crisis of the nation's history; though the subsequent popularity of the book is more significant still, while it has also supplied materials for discussion to the majority of later publicists.

Synthesis and Condemnation of Italian History

FEDERICO CHABOD

One of the outstanding Italian scholars of our day is Federico Chabod, Professor of Modern History at the University of Rome. His brilliant work in many areas of European history has established him as a worthy successor to his great mentor, Benedetto Croce. At the present time Chabod is an editor of the *Rivista Storica Italiana,* as well as director of the Croce Institute of Historical Study in Naples, and president of the Bureau of the International Committee of Historical Sciences. He is the author of numerous books and articles on the Renaissance and modern history, including a multi-volume study of Italian foreign policy, *Storia della politica estera italiana dal 1870 al 1896* (the first volume of which appeared in 1951), and an editor of the *Documenti diplomatici italiani.* The following selection is from his "Del 'Principe' di Niccolò Machiavelli," which was first published in the *Nuova Rivista Storica,* Vol. IX (1925).

MACHIAVELLI CONSIDERED AGAINST THE BACKGROUND OF HIS TIME

Basing his doctrine, then, on the present state of Italian history, which he expounds with unwonted clarity, Machiavelli also accepts its premises. In creating the Principate, regarded as the expression of an individual virtue that is extraneous to the life of the masses, he confirms the death-sentence pronounced on contemporary society, which, viewed as a political force capable of revival, is dissociated from the reconstruction of the State. Everything is dependent on the shrewdness and energy of the lonely *condottiere.*

This lack of confidence in the people, this grievous condemnation of contemporary society is implicit in the very creation of the Prince. We find the author breaking off in the middle of a passionate, hitherto uninterrupted evaluation of the energies of a people that discovers the springs of its greatness within itself (this evaluation is marked by sudden slight hesitations, which leave the writer at times incapable, after his initial act of faith in the virtue of the

people, of deciding between the mob and the individual, and lead him to interrupt his eulogy of the people's struggle against the patricians with an examination of the ways in which the Prince can avoid the vice of ingratitude). We find him suddenly returning to motifs adumbrated earlier, making them the basis of a lengthy discourse and investing them with an unsuspected vitality. We find him abandoning his comprehensive survey of the past and carrying out a minute and subtle analysis whose purpose is to determine a new social system. These procedures would suffice in themselves to reveal Niccolò's state of mind when, having laid aside his curial robes, he finds himself confronted again and again with the obtrusive problem of the reorganization of present-day life — a problem which had already tormented him during his years of public service, and which is now aggravated by considerations of a practical nature.

As he contemplates the Italy of his day Machiavelli is filled with a profound sense of grief. At times this becomes crystallized,

From Federico Chabod, *Machiavelli and the Renaissance.* Translated by David Moore. (London: Bowes & Bowes Publishers Ltd., 1958; Cambridge, Mass.: Harvard University Press, 1959), pp. 79–84, 95–105. Reprinted by permission of the publishers and the Società Editrice Dante Alighieri.

and finds an outlet now in invective, now in sarcasm, now in the sudden cry of distress,[1] while at other times the sad-eyed writer indulges in vain regrets. At intervals he becomes impatient of the chains that bind him and wants to burst them, dragging with him his fellow-citizens, but he soon relapses into his former state, surveying them with a sad irony in which there is all the disillusionment of the man who yearns for action and is forced to confine himself exclusively to flights of fancy.

To him Florence is an object of pity, so much so that at times his old affection for his native city seems almost to have deserted him. The much-discussed epigram about Pier Soderini is merely the concrete expression of an attitude of mind. This was formerly characterized by passion and indignation but now these give way to a mocking irony, which, however, is tempered with a note of grief when he comes to recognize the futility of his anguish.

Here in Florence there has never been any organized political life. The Republic of Soderini, even though the writer had no small stake in it, is deemed weak and inept, because the Florentine *bourgeoisie,* the raw material of the State, is as corrupt as all the rest of Italian society. The barely perceptible, sarcastic smile of pity which Machiavelli cannot keep from his lips and eyes when he speaks of Savonarola (to him, as to Commynes, Savonarola is a *bon homme,* except that for the somewhat bewildered sincerity of the Frenchman Mach-

iavelli substitutes the slyness and subtlety of a Florentine) reveals to us without need of comment the true impression which this crumbling society makes upon the Secretary.

Not even Venice, dear though she is to the hearts of the Republicans of Florence, offers him any grounds for hope. There, indeed, he sees not the resplendent glory of the lion of St. Mark but the profound weakness of a State which, living in isolation within the narrow circle of a mercantile oligarchy, cannot achieve internal security, and, when it desires to widen the boundaries of its domain, going outside its natural small field of political expansion, is faced with certain ruin. The marvellous economic power of the Venetian Republic does not suffice to create political virtue. Machiavelli, who has little regard for the one, looks in vain for the other; and he bitterly castigates Venice for her efforts to achieve hegemony, efforts that still reverberate in the memories of Florentine politicians, stunned by the unexpected disaster of Vailate.

Milan and Naples are rotten to the core; Genoa is worthless; and Italy, taken as a whole, is the most corrupt of nations. Niccolò is quite convinced of it!

But what prompts this harsh, categorical verdict of political weakness, which as a statement of fact is only partly true?

Sometimes Machiavelli has a clear vision of some of the chief reasons for the failure of the Communal system. In a wonderful passage in the *Florentine Histories* he succeeds to a great extent in solving the mystery of that civilization's evolution, indicating one of the points at which it was rotten,[2] and at other times themes of astonishing amplitude and profundity enter into his historical vision. But these are sudden flashes of insight that come to the author in the midst of his rapt meditations, which

---

[1] ". . . but he who was born in Italy or Greece, and has not become, in Italy a Transalpine, in Greece a Turk, has cause to denounce his age and to extol the past. For there are many things about the past that make it marvellous; but as to the present, there is nothing that redeems it from every extremity of wretchedness, infamy and shame. There is no observance of religion or law, there is no military consciousness. Instead, it is defiled by every species of abomination" (*Discorsi,* Preface to Book II). "As for the union of the other Italians, you make me laugh — first, because no union will ever be able to do any good . . . secondly, because the head and the tail are not coordinated; nor will this generation ever move a step, for whatever cause . . ." (*Lettere Familiari,* CXXXI, dated 10 August, 1513).

[2] "The bitter and natural enmities that exist between the masses and the nobles . . . are the cause of all the evils that arise in cities; for from this diversity of humours spring all the other things that disturb the peace of Republics" (*Florentine Histories,* III, i).

range over the whole vast course of history. When he has to condescend to a more specific judgment on this or that Italian State — and above all when the regenerative purpose that proceeds from his will seeks to reconcile itself with the creative act of his spirit, and Niccolò no longer moves about amid the quiet of his peaceful and secluded study, but ventures forth into the living world of his time — then it is that his thought loses this breadth of vision. From the consideration of social problems, from the unhealthy party feuds and fruitless struggles between people and nobles his mind turns to the infamies of the mercenary troops, the inertia of the princes, and the weakness of republics that lack armies of their own. To his mind the principal cause of Italy's misfortune is her lack of a national militia. Forgetting the more intimate processes of popular feeling, he concentrates entirely on the visible acts of violence perpetrated by the base and contemptible mercenaries and on the folly of rulers who do not even know how to control their forces. In all his writings he constantly bewails and denounces the indolence of leaders and soldiers, the cause of Italy's present woes; and he never ceases to execrate in turn the bad military organization of the republics and the mean outlook of the hired troops. The militia is not only the foundation of the new structure that Niccolò desires to raise: it becomes in its turn a criterion of history. . . .

THE NEW SEIGNEUR AND
MACHIAVELLI'S NEW ILLUSION

Thus the intellectual world from which the Prince emerges is entirely political and military in character. The life of the people has ceased to command the writer's attention; and since Court life and martial activity find their expression in the man who presides over them and are epitomized in a specific human figure, it is the princes of Italy who become responsible for their country's ruin.

But since the cause of error is in them, in them will be the remedy. And while Savonarola, who regarded Princes as the fountain of all wickedness and believed that they were sent by God to punish the sins of their subjects, sought to reconstruct his world by expelling them from society, Niccolò focuses his attention upon them to the exclusion of all else.

Thus there emerges the new Seigneur.

On a number of previous occasions Machiavelli had expressed his faith in individual virtue as the power which could lift the masses from their degradation and restore good institutions; already he had believed in it as being the key to the State's salvation. Even when his imagination dwells upon the complex life of the people of Rome he sees this isolated quality as an organizing force; it nearly always reappears, and its presence within the fuller and more varied life of the people is reaffirmed. Here Machiavelli is adapting himself to the facts of Italian history and accepting the doctrine of the Renaissance. In his affirmation of individual virtue Niccolò reveals the same human limitations as Guicciardini. But at other times the theme of the virtue of the Man alternates with that of good institutions. Regenerative power no longer resides only in the mind of an individual. It is inherent also in the very strength of the laws, that is to say in the vitality of the people, who find within themselves the goodness and the discipline that will enable them to make a fresh start, to recover their greatness. And now the new law-giver does not develop into a tyrant, but is content to recall the city to the paths of righteousness and to restore to it all its ancient institutions.

Sometimes, indeed, Niccolò hesitates. Not that he does not believe in virtue, not that he has lost faith in the ability of the Man to conquer and rule; but this ability seems to him too dependent on the whims of fortune, too closely bound up with the precariousness of human existence. True, this hesitation does not yet altogether reflect the new consciousness which enables the thinker to see how vain is individual effort when the foundation is lacking and the *condottiere's* actions do not find an adequate counterpart in the spiritual life of the people; and often his doubt has a particular reason, and is not due to a sudden change of thought, so that he thinks that if human life were longer, or virtue could be handed down together with authority, virtue alone would suffice to maintain a State. But in spite of this Machiavelli still pauses. Perhaps the new man has his origin in this conflict between the citizen of the Renaissance and the thinker, who at certain moments is in advance of his age.

But now his doubts cease. Good institutions are lost from sight, as is the notion of a return to the principle that determines the organization of a republic. The spotlight is focused on the virtue of the Prince, who must breathe life into his inert material through the compelling power of his will. City, people, good institutions, a return to the principles which would make it possible to reorganize society on its original basis — all these things are far from Machiavelli's thoughts. He is concerned with his own age, and seeks to imbue it with a new vigour. In the fever of creation he forgets his conflicts, his intellectual hesitations, his early doubts about the organizing capacity of the Man, who is a product of recent Italian history. This Man reappears at the last, all alone in his armour — shrewd in diplomatic manoeuvre, fortified with every sort of civic wisdom, purged of every weakness. He is the redeemer, who will atone for the sins of former Seigneurs by his glory — the glory of a new Prince.

And Machiavelli did not realize that even such a reconstruction as this was a vain dream, that this was his last and greatest illusion.

All of the vital forces of the nation were in process of dissolution, and no new force had so far appeared. The Communal *bourgeoisie* no longer had the energy to support the burden of government, and signs of a new consciousness, of a new class capable of replacing it were lacking. The provinces were still disunited and fragmentary; every day they were being further weakened, politically and economically, by the pres-

sure of the great Western States. Literature and humanism had deprived the people of their sense of moral values and social necessities, though they still retained their individualistic tendencies. To believe that a military leader could revive the declining fortunes of Italy and constitute a State which neither the transcendent vitality of the Communes nor the unitarian resolve of the great Seigneurs of the Trecento had been able to integrate; to imagine that it was enough simply to adopt a new principle of leadership and to reform the militia, that to this end actions inspired by a single will, the acute insight into events, resourcefulness, and severity of a supreme seigneur were sufficient to prop up or rather to reconstruct that which was bound to collapse in the nature of things, so that an entire epoch of history should have a fitting climax — this was a beautiful, audacious, formidable dream, but it *was* a dream!

And the Machiavelli who, intoxicated by the glory of the Roman people, condemns Caesar, errs now when he forecasts miracles to be wrought by the hand of Valentino or one of the Medici; for their efforts, however admirable in point of administrative sagacity, could not have launched Italian society on to paths different from those along which it was naturally travelling with catastrophic speed. If he heeded the advice and warning of Niccolò the Prince would have had to deny the results of two hundred years of history; he would have had to direct the stream of events into different channels from those which it was destined to follow. And if at first his impassioned vision of the people and their healthy strength prompts him to condemn the "tyrant" (and what a tyrant!), his yearning for an Italy imbued with a new vigour, capacity, and freedom subsequently prevents him from accurately assessing the worth of the "little castle" that he has built amid the tormenting anxiety of his unhappy leisure.

Carried away by the fervour of his feeling and imagination, Machiavelli in the end contradicts himself. His theoretical pessimism suddenly changes into a boundless confidence not only in the statesman but also in the nation that awaits its redeemer and is all ready to follow him. In this way it reveals itself as nothing more than an intellectual attitude, incapable of resisting the impact of emotion.[3] His scepticism is transformed into a heart-cry of hope and faith; and his words of contempt for Man, who is in himself a base creature, become an invocation, which assumes a religious tone and contains an echo from the Scriptures.

But even when the idea of a "national army" holds his attention Niccolò fails to perceive the absurd errors into which he falls. To make the security of the State the responsibility of all, not only of the city-dwellers but also of the poor inhabitants of the outlying districts, forcing them to share the heaviest task which men can be called upon to shoulder on behalf of the community; to interest all those who live in a territory in its safety and integrity; to look for the foundation of social life in the duty of all when confronted by the enemy — this was to effect a radical change not only in the military system but in the political and moral system too. In other words, it was to step outside the context of history, that history to which even the writer looked for guidance throughout his work of political theorization.

Machiavelli shuts his eyes to this. When he is concerned with the practice of government the necessity of prompt action prevents him from perceiving the connection between the instructions issued to the discontented Communes and his own concept of

[3] And herein lies the difference between the pessimism of Machiavelli and that of Guicciardini. In the former, intensity of feeling often succeeds in making nonsense of the theoretical assertion, so that men whom his intellect despises regain his confidence. In the latter, the theoretical assertion, even if it is less pungent, is perfectly consistent with his emotional indifference; hence Messer Francesco not only speaks of the "people" as a crazy animal, but, in conformity with his thought, takes good care not to associate with them. He is haughty, as his contemporaries note, whereas Machiavelli is amiable toward his friends and in everyday life just an ordinary man of the people.

the militia as the bulwark of the country, while as Secretary of the Nine he sanctions the dismemberment and the essential division of the State and countenances the distrust that exists between one village and another, and between the villages in general and the mother city. But this is not all. Even later, when he reduces his original practical plan to a theoretical form, he is unconscious of the decidedly revolutionary character with which he is investing not only the military system but the whole body politic.

He will speculate at length as to the correct method of "swearing-in soldiers"; and he will endeavour to find out what religion has the power to make men face death with serenity. But meanwhile he bases the new principate on the idea of his own army, without realizing that this idea is the most flagrant and irremediable contradiction that can be imagined of his political programme. It always remains a mystery to him that if the soldiers are to be made to take a proper oath they need a religion which he does not offer them, and that before demanding sacrifices it is necessary to create a social consciousness, at least on a regional basis, and a political spirit deriving from the realization, however confused, that the passions of rulers are indissolubly bound up with the passions of their subjects.

Nor does he ask himself whether it is actually in the interest of the sovereign of a large and powerful State to create a citizen militia, which would need so many months of training to be capable of withstanding effectively the impact of powerful mercenaries that the efficacy and above all the timeliness of the remedy would be open to question; or whether it becomes the absolute head of a State to put weapons into the hands of subjects who might in many cases use them to drive him from his ducal palace.

When his thought takes this turn, when he finds himself faced with this profound spiritual crisis, from which he might emerge perhaps without hope, but with his powers of judgment enhanced, Machiavelli stops in mid-career, and continues to confine himself to the details of the question. He devotes all his energies to technical analysis, without perceiving the connection between this and the general organization of the State.

In constructing his principate he completely discounts the people as a creative force, but he soon recalls them when he has need of their moral support. The general framework and the new prop are not of the same metal, and they do not go well together. But Niccolò does not notice this, and with touching pertinacity he tries to bolster up an edifice that is destined to be brought down by the first violent gust of wind.

The contradiction is inevitable because it is implicit in the premises — because, essentially, Machiavelli wants a national militia inasmuch as he finds that the cause of Italy's ruins lies in her military corruption: once this has been remedied everything will be all right again. And so we find him concentrating on the remedy *per se* to the exclusion of all else, oblivious of the profound changes that it brings about in the material to which it is applied, and of the strength of tissue that is still required if it is not to prove too drastic.

But it is also inevitable because, in demanding that arms should be entrusted to the actual inhabitants of a town, Machiavelli becomes once again a municipalist, a descendant of the old *bourgeoisie* of the free Communes. He is now not a prophet of the future, but simply an anachronistic evoker of a past that must be regarded as dead.[4] He is unaware of the sentiment that prompts him, and believes that he is preaching a new doctrine of salvation, whereas

he is in fact repeating old phrases that have come back into circulation in these disastrous times; and he himself does not even heed the fact that in so doing he is reverting to the habits of thought current in the palmy days of Savonarola and, unconsciously or not, reviving the fundamental ideas of that age. Long study of the military greatness of republican Rome has renewed his confidence: we are suddenly confronted once more with the citizen of Florence, who contradicts the instructor of the new Prince.

And so that vague confidence in the people — stronger than any theoretical pessimism — which is essential if they are to be entrusted with arms, remains an ingenuous and obscure sentiment: the writer is not yet capable either of clarifying in his own mind the motives by which he is actuated or of avoiding contradictions. It is true that among Machiavelli's writings *The Art of War* most nearly approaches the *Discorsi* in spirit, and that in *The Prince* itself the chapters that most of all remind us of the great commentary on Livy are precisely those which deal with the military constitution of the new State; yet there is here only a part of the thought of the *Discorsi*, only a facet of the strength with which the Roman world was imbued. When he returns to his own age and assumes the specific rôle of reformer Niccolò thinks that he is making a new and vital contribution but does not succeed in developing it to the full. His experience can suggest to his mind a tentative scheme of political reorganization, but this is still limited to a particular field; and when that experience is confronted with the world of the Renaissance it is inadequate to inform

4 Those who have looked upon Machiavelli as the herald of the modern age have been guilty of a gross error. The Florentine Secretary's "armed people" is merely a momentary and futile reincarnation of the old Communal militias (whatever the technical modifications necessarily introduced). Modern compulsory military service, apart from all the variations of detail, which are neither small nor trivial, is based on such a different conception of the internal political constitution

of the State that any comparison is impossible. To be the true prophet of our times Machiavelli would have had to modify not only the military system but also, theoretically at least, the political system against the general background of which alone the individual reforms which he proposed should be considered; but that would be asking too much. Certain it is, however, that he who in his political thought was a man of the Renaissance became a man of the thirteenth century when he turned his attention to military matters.

it with all the motifs which it should embrace.

Restricted, then, by limitations of thought which he is unable to overcome, Niccolò creates his Principate without perceiving the uselessness of his labours; and amid the frenzy of his unbridled passion he gives himself up to his creative vision without measuring precisely its concrete worth. *The Prince,* a theoretical picture and epitome of the outcome of Italian history, is also animated by a vain hope: the Seigneurs of Italy have consigned that hope to oblivion.

But this very fact lends a singular importance to the little treatise. We are conscious at every step of a desperate effort to prop up that which must surely collapse, of a tragic attempt to build in a vacuum, of the unleashing of an emotion which ultimately colours the analysis and attains the grandeur of a religious warning. And it is not without a feeling of sadness that we contemplate the formidable labours of a peerless intellect which seeks with passionate faith to arouse the Redeemer and fails to perceive how its very creativeness makes manifest the disintegration of the material which it vainly wishes to imbue with virtue. Other works, at first sight more deceptive, reveal that in the Europe of those days new seeds of life were germinating. This one, on the other hand, so infinitely superior to all others in virtue of its imaginative power and dramatic emphasis, testifies to the passing of a glorious era that has run its course.

Thus *The Prince* is at once a synthesis and a condemnation of two centuries of Italian history; and far more than its supposed immorality, what should have stirred the emotions of the commentators was the thought of the boundless misery which was overtaking our civilization.

Machiavelli's Historical Method and Statecraft

HERBERT BUTTERFIELD

Herbert Butterfield, who is a professor of modern history at Cambridge University and Master of Peterhouse, is one of the best-known contemporary historians. His remarkable and stimulating contributions to the early history of science, to English history and historiography, and to many other areas of historical study are widely read and respected. He holds honorary doctorate degrees from five universities, and from 1938 to 1952 was editor of the *Cambridge Historical Journal*. Among Butterfield's many significant publications are: *The Whig Interpretation of History* (1931); *The Origins of Modern Science* (1949 and 1957); *Christianity and History* (1949); *Man on His Past* (1955); and *George III and the Historians* (1957).

I F the new science of statecraft had its origin, on the one hand, in the dispatches and state papers of government servants, it is connected also, on another side, with the development of historical study and the rise of the Florentine school of historians. If there are passages in Machiavelli's letters which might have been part of his treatises on politics, there are also passages in his *History of Florence* which might have occurred in either. It was a time when the writers of history were often also administrators or diplomatists versed in government and public affairs; and the historians of this period in Florence seemed to show a special interest in the events that were nearly contemporary. They brought their practical experience and their love of political discussion into their historical inquiries — trying to seize upon faults in policy, or to explain a political decision or a military defeat. Machiavelli's criticism in *The Prince* of the conduct of Louis XII during the second French invasion, can be paralleled by Guicciardini's comments, scattered more diffusely in his narrative of the wars. There was a further reason why these writers were so able to regard recent events in a light that

was at the same time practical and historical. It is surprising to what an extent the Italians of these days felt that their world had been shaken and cut in two by the invasion of 1494. Guicciardini, setting out in his history to give "an account of the troubles in Italy together with the causes from which so many evils were derived," opened his narrative with the words:

It is certain that, for above a thousand years — since the Roman Empire, weakened by a change in her ancient institutions, began to decline from the height of grandeur to which amazing virtue and good fortune had helped to bring her — Italy had at no time enjoyed a state of such complete prosperity and repose, as in the year 1490, and some time before and after.

The consciousness that the year 1494 had opened the gates to disasters which had tormented Italy ever since, was a great incentive to historical inquiry and political analysis in other people besides Machiavelli; and the country seemed moved, as we were moved after the War of 1914, to enter upon a more intensive self-examination. But Machiavelli distinguished himself by claiming that in the study of history one could discover not only the causes but also

From Herbert Butterfield, *The Statecraft of Machiavelli*, (London: G. Bell & Sons, Ltd., 1955), pp. 26–41, 89–94. Reprinted by permission of the publishers.

the cure of the ills of the time. Where he was peculiar, where he provoked the criticism of Guicciardini, and where he earnestly desired to convert the Italians of his day, was in his attitude to historical study — his peculiar views concerning the utility of history. His position was based upon the combination of certain theories, each of which, taken separately, was perhaps not uncommon in sixteenth-century Italy — theories which Guicciardini himself held in a certain manner and even would express in very similar terms; though Guicciardini did not apprehend them with the same rigidity, or accept them in the same way as the basis of further inference — did not admit that a science of statecraft could be founded on them or that Machiavelli was justified in the combination that he made of these views. The theories in question were first of all a doctrine of "imitation," which conditioned Machiavelli's attitude to the great men of the past; secondly an important thesis concerning historical recurrence, one that affected therefore the problem of the deduction of general laws from historical data; and thirdly a conviction of the superiority of the ancient world as a guide to human behavior in the present. These three aspects of Machiavelli's thought represent what perhaps were the most typical features in Renaissance theory on the subject of the past. But in Machiavelli they acquired new power by their combination — reinforcing one another by their mutual interactions. They gave, indeed, a peculiar shape to his doctrine concerning the utility of history.

The doctrine of imitation, applied particularly to the example of great men, appears on numerous occasions and can be found in various passages of The Prince. It can be seen in the dedication of this book and also in the address in the final chapter. The general thesis is most clearly stated in Chapter VI:

Nobody must be surprised if in my discussion of new principalities . . . I make reference to very imposing examples; for as men nearly always follow the path traced by others and proceed in their actions by imitation — though they cannot quite keep to the path or reach the full merits of those whom they imitate — a prudent man ought always to walk in the path traced out by great men and imitate those who are most excellent, so that if he does not attain their prowess he may at least achieve something of the flavour of it.

The actual workings of this principle are apparent in some such passages as the following, which is from the Discourses of Livy:

Those who wish to learn the method to adopt for the achievement of this end, need not take any more trouble than to put before their eyes the lives of good men, such as Timoleon the Corinthian, Aratus the Sicyonian, and the like; in whose lives they will see so much mutual confidence and satisfaction existing between the people governing and the people governed, that they will desire to imitate the conduct of these men, which they will find to be an easy matter.

Disc. III, 5

Constantly we meet sentences like the following, from the Art of War:

If then our princes would read and duly consider the lives and fortunes of these great men, one would think it impossible that they should not alter their conduct.

The second of Machiavelli's theses was based on the view that human nature is unchanging throughout the ages. Human passions, being constant, move men at all periods to the same kinds of action, driving the story to the same crises and conjunctures; so that history tends to fall into repeating patterns, instead of progressing to an unforeseeable future that is pregnant with hidden shapes. In other words, the course of history does not generate new things, and with all its host of accidents and incidents, the world throughout the centuries remains essentially the same; events occur in only a limited number of combinations; and historical situations perpetually repeat themselves, dissolving for a season but then re-forming after the ancient pattern. On this view of history change is kaleidoscopic — there is reshuffling and recombination but no transformation of the constituent parts; historical change is not regarded as the process of an evolutionary development in which each stage of the story means attainment of something new. Machiavelli holds this view of historical recurrence with a certain rigidity; he is not content (as we perhaps should be) to say that, at certain periods of the past, situations and events provided mere analogies with things that we know in the present. Guicciardini, as we might expect, showed the greater elasticity in this matter, though stating the doctrine of historical recurrence in terms very similar to those of Machiavelli himself. Guicciardini, indeed, stressed a different aspect of the topic, insisting, as we have already seen, upon the complexity of historical change. He notes that every episode involves factors which make it not quite like any historical parallels that can be adduced. He emphasizes the view that each historical episode is unique in some way; each must be treated therefore as a special case. So, while Guicciardini says that too much must not be made of historical examples, Machiavelli on the other hand uses the doctrine of historical recurrence with remarkable effect. It enables him to go to history for the discovery of general rules and political precepts, and he can regard these as possessing universal validity, since they have reference to conjunctures that are always likely to recur.

His view can be illustrated from a passage which is taken from the *Discourses*:

Whoever considers things present and things past will easily understand how the same appetites and humours are and always have been incident to all states and people, so that by diligently examining the course of former ages it is an easy matter for men to foresee what is going to happen in any commonwealth, and not only to provide such remedies against future evils as their predecessors did, but (if there be no precedent) to strike out new ones on the basis of the existing analogies. But since considerations of this kind are too often neglected or little understood, or are beyond the knowl-

edge of those men who govern states, it comes to pass that the same evils and inconveniences take place in all ages of history.

Disc. I, 39

Towards the close of the same work there is an even stronger statement of the thesis:

Wise men say (and perhaps not unjustly) that in order to form an impression of what is yet to come, we ought to consider what is already passed; for there is nothing in this world at present, or at any other time, but has and will have its counterpart in antiquity; which happens because these things are operated by human beings who, having the same passions in all ages, must necessarily behave uniformly in similar situations.

Disc. III, 43

Accepting the fact that men are alike and that they tend to imitate one another, Machiavelli asks that this imitation shall become conscious and shall be an imitation of the best. Accepting the fact that events are for ever repeating themselves, he insists that we shall take advantage of it, read history, and learn the best that has been done in previous cycles. He required only one further stage of reasoning to bring his views to that point of rigidity which gives the lessons of history their greatest simplification; and that was the addition of the final thesis that there was one particular period of history so noteworthy in its success and happiness — one particular cycle which had so long cheated the inevitable process toward corruption — that the modern world could do nothing better than accept it as the pattern for its own conduct, not merely seeking to recapture its prevailing spirit, but copying its methods in the concrete, piece by piece. It was avowedly upon the imitation of antiquity — though an antiquity interpreted by him, whether he knew it or not, in the light of contemporary Italian situations and needs — that he based his new science of politics and took up a particular position in which he seems to have regarded himself as standing against the world.

His attitude toward his science of statecraft is explained in the place where we should most expect to find the exposition of his fundamental conception — in the Introduction to Book I of the *Discourses,* which represented his most elaborate political work. It is here that he makes his claim to originality and if his views are considered in the light of the historical principles that have just been set forward, it will be seen why his friend Nardi, on hearing readings from the *Discourses,* declared that the work was "of new argument, never attempted by any other man, so far as I know." It will be seen why Machiavelli himself, in the Dedicatory Letter to the *Discourses,* could write:

Although, owing to the envious nature of men, it is always as dangerous to discover new orderings and ways as to explore unknown lands and seas — for human beings are always more ready to blame than to praise the actions of their fellows — nevertheless. . . I have resolved to enter upon a path that has not yet been trodden by human foot.

The Introduction makes reference to the veneration with which classical works of art are regarded by Machiavelli's contemporaries — "how often it happens (to omit other instances) that an immense price is given by the curious for a fragment of an old statue that will serve as an adornment for a cabinet or a model for artists"; and Machiavelli comments on the trouble which artists are willing to take in order to come up to the standard of classical works which they have adopted as their pattern. He goes on to show how lawyers take their precepts and doctors borrow their remedies from the practitioners of the ancient world; "in civil differences, as well as in the various maladies that are incident to mankind, we always have recourse to such decisions and prescriptions as have been handed down to us from our ancestors." Yet, he says, the "deeds of former kings, generals, citizens, 'Legislators,' etc. are now rather admired than adopted for imitation":

In establishing a republic, in maintaining a state, in governing a kingdom, in organizing an army and conducting a war, in administering a subject people, in extending an empire, there is neither prince nor republic, nor general nor citizen who makes reference to the precedents in antiquity. . . The cause of this is the lack of a true understanding of history — the failure to take from history that significance and appreciate that wisdom which it contains. Those who read it and delight to hear the varieties of incident which it narrates, do so without dreaming of taking examples for imitation . . . Desiring however to induce men to forsake this error I have thought it necessary to write a commentary upon those books of Titus Livius which have been spared us by the malevolence of time. I shall refer to both ancient and modern affairs in order that these books may be better understood; so that those who read these Discourses may reap that advantage which ought to be their object when they come to the study of history.

Ten years before he had begun writing his books, Machiavelli had stated the whole thesis in similar terms in a small treatise on the *Method of dealing with the rebels of the Val di Chiana.* Here he writes:

I have heard it said that history is the master of our actions and especially of the policy of princes; and the world was always inclined to sameness, inhabited as it is by men who in all ages have the same passions. Always there were the men who served and the men who had command; men who gladly served and men who served with a bad will. . . So, if it is true that history is the master of our actions, it would have been useful if the men who had to chastise and administer the district of Valdichiana had taken example from those who were masters of the world and had imitated their actions, especially in a case in which there was a clear precedent concerning the conduct to pursue.

Earlier than this, on 21st November 1500, he had shown that he intended this teaching to be followed by practical statesmen; for commenting on Louis XII's invasion of Italy, he had said: "His Majesty ought to follow the methods of those who in past times have wished to possess a foreign province"; and he had put forward some of the maxims which were to be learned from history — maxims later elaborated in *The Prince* and further expanded in the *Discourses*. And according to this latter work, where the source of the maxims is more clearly revealed, it is evident that, on Machiavelli's view, Louis XII, when he desired conquests in Italy, ought to have "got up the subject" of foreign conquest by historical study and followed the examples of the ancient Romans.

It is a mistake to water down the meaning of the very passage in which Machiavelli states — as indeed on many other occasions — the fundamental point of his new science. It is wrong to imagine that he was merely pleading for the growth of wisdom, the widening of experience which may come to any man from historical study; or to think that he would have been satisfied to see his contemporaries vaguely inspired with the idea of conducting themselves like Romans. The analogies that he makes — the artist copying classical models, the physician taking his prescriptions, the lawyer following ancient laws — are very striking; and to these may be added the case of the art of war where Machiavelli's principle of direct imitation is most marked. His attitude to history and antiquity implied in him a preoccupation with concrete cases and practical instances — an emphasis upon history as a storehouse of examples rather than a field of experience in a more elastic sense of the words. And this is in keeping with many of his habitual statements — his very vocabulary and his *clichés* — when he is speaking of the lessons of the past. His doctrine of imitation does in fact mean the imitation of definite specimens of successful policy, with a particular stress on the actions of great men and on the examples of antiquity. Speaking roughly and stating the case perhaps at its crudest, we may say that the position he takes up rests on the view that if a certain expedient has proved successful in some conjuncture in the past, the trick ought not to be forgotten in a world in which historical situations are being constantly repeated. Studying history in examples, Machiavelli draws lessons

from striking incidents, and catches the very tones of the schoolteacher who rounds off the story with a moral — saying perpetually: "From this short narrative we may observe. . ."; "It behoves all princes, therefore"; "whoever reads this passage will see how necessary it is" — and then will follow some political maxim. Guicciardini, therefore, is really attacking the view of Machiavelli when he urges that it is not useful to make deductions from particular examples, and says that a very small modification of circumstances makes the historical precedent inapplicable. History does not quite repeat itself, he maintains, and every example in history has features which make it a special case.

Machiavelli, then, hoped by the study of antiquity to discover practical precepts and definite rules of political action, doing this specifically, as physicians and lawyers were in the habit of doing when they needed fresh remedies or principles of law. If he had intended anything short of this he would hardly have had to complain of the indifference of his contemporaries in Renaissance Italy to the examples of ancient Rome. Nor would Guicciardini have criticized his position — sharing, as he did, the general admiration for the Roman practice, but repudiating the idea that sixteenth-century statesmen should attempt to copy it in detail.

How greatly do these men deceive themselves who at every point quote the example of the Romans [said Guicciardini]. It would be necessary to have a state under the same conditions as theirs, before one could take them as the model for political action.

Imitating the Romans, he argued, was only to be compared with the spectacle of the ass trying to run in a horse race. In military matters he ridiculed Machiavelli's curious disparagement of fire-arms — merely because the Romans did not make war with gunpowder! And while Machiavelli complained of those who questioned the authority of Livy, as though he were the inventor of "idle stories," Guicciardini expressed a certain scepticism not only concerning Livy but also on the subject of historians in general. If we can take the appeal to the classical world as a parallel to the Protestant regard for the authority of the Bible, Guicciardini represents the free or modernist view — and indeed it is not to be considered that any man of those days would have rejected the authority of the ancients altogether — but Machiavelli is the "fundamentalist," the devotee of "verbal inspiration," more slavish than his political contemporaries in his reverence for the statecraft of the ancient world.

Upon this topic he is most militant in his writings, most conscious that he diverges from the majority of his contemporaries. And not only does he despise the statecraft of his epoch, but repeatedly he shows that the seat of their error lies precisely here. In the Preface to the second book of the *Discourses* he sets out to defend himself against the criticism that he is one of the men who blindly praise the ancients and blindly disparage the present time.

I do not know if I deserve to be numbered amongst those who deceive themselves [he writes] when in my discourses I praise the antique Roman times so much, while condemning the contemporary age. And, in truth, if the virtue which then prevailed and the vice which reigns today were not more clear than the sun, I should proceed in a more restrained manner in order to prevent myself from falling into that kind of self-deception. . . But since the thing is so manifest that every person with eyes can see it, I shall let myself go and make no bones about what I believe on the subject of the past and the present; so that the minds of the young who may read my writings, may shun the latter and prepare to imitate the former, whenever fortune shall give them the opportunity.

Machiavelli's science of statecraft claimed to combine the lessons of history, the wisdom of the ancients, and the examples of the noble and great. But he did not reckon for the personal equation and in reality no political teaching has been identified more

closely with the single personality of its author. Today we regard the statecraft which he imputed to antiquity as a signal product of the Renaissance mind. It is a warning to all who hope to discover the "lessons of history." The mind of the sixteenth-century politician caught from the past the episodes that were analogous to those of its own world; valued in ancient heroes the qualities that would have been effective in Renaissance Italy; and took from history only the things it could recognize and ratify and applaud. Much of Machiavelli's teaching, therefore, is his own, in spite of himself: and we can regard it in part as the historical product of his particular world.

Machiavelli was specially interested in what we today might call the pathology of states, the seamy side of policy, the conduct of government under emergency conditions. His maxims were very often addressed to a ruler in the anomalous position of a Catherine de Medici, rather than to a ruler in the more established position of a Philip II of Spain. They postulate — and to a historian they reveal — the adventurous character of Renaissance politics. Machiavelli indeed has little to say about normal governments in ordinary happy times. What he does say on a number of occasions is that for these governments no problem really exists. "How easy a matter it is to conduct affairs when the people are not corrupted," he will say in the *Discourses*; and in another place he remarks: "For when people are well governed they neither seek nor welcome any change of government." He instances those Roman emperors "who had no need for either Praetorian bands or a multitude of legions to defend them; because their own goodness and the affection of the senate and the people were a sufficient defence." When he has set out to prove that "if one weak prince should succeed another, it is impossible to maintain any state," he adds, "unless as in the case of France, it is supported by virtue of its ancient laws and fundamental constitutions."

In the second chapter of *The Prince*, Machiavelli tells us:

I say, therefore, that in hereditary states, accustomed to the reigning family, the difficulty of maintaining them is far less than in new monarchies; for it is sufficient not to exceed the ancestral usages and to accommodate oneself to accidental circumstances; so that a prince of this kind, if of ordinary ability, will always be able to maintain his position in a state, unless some very exceptional and overwhelming force deprives him of it; and even if he is thus deprived of it, as soon as the new occupier comes into any kind of difficulty, he will be able to regain it.

A little later he says of the legitimate prince that "unless extraordinary vices make him hated, it is only reasonable for his subjects to be naturally attached to him." And the following chapter opens: "But it is in the new monarchy that difficulties really exist." After a number of chapters dealing specifically with various kinds of new monarchy and the problems that concern these, Machiavelli may give a good deal of advice that can be applied to ancient and established governments; but he is dealing with topics, like the military question, which obviously cannot avoid being of interest to legitimate princes as well as new ones. Even so, he makes a remark at times which implies that it is really the usurper or the "new monarch" that he has in mind. He will note the fact that what he has to say is applicable to legitimate princes as well as illegitimate. He will point out a procedure that is necessary for old princes and then use the argument *a fortiori* of new ones. He will explain that the Ottoman Empire is not a valid example of a new monarchy, because, though the prince himself may be "new" and may not have risen to the throne by direct hereditary succession, the rules of the state are old and the people are "ready to receive him as if he were their hereditary lord." When he quotes the example of Ferdinand of Aragon he shows why Ferdinand may for special reasons almost be taken as an example of a "new" prince. And altogether his advice is directed to the adventurer, the self-made man, governing under emergency conditions, rather than to the traditional monarch, secure in the love of his subjects and sufficiently guided by the ancestral usages of his house. When in Chapter XXIV he refers to all this which has preceded, he expounds what is the real purpose of his book:

The things which are written above, if they are prudently observed, will make a new prince seem like an hereditary ruler and will render him at once more secure and firm in the state than if he had been established there of old.

Then in his magnificent final chapter, he opens with the question: "Whether at present the time is not propitious in Italy for a new prince." Machiavelli was offering an infallible guide for new princes, who wished to become as safe as old ones. In our age he might have called his book "The Prince: a text-book for usurpers."

The maxims in the *Discourses* do not generally deal with what we should call the problems of normal political life. A large number of them, particularly in the first book, are rules to be observed by the "Legislator" – the "new prince," who is to found a state upon the basis of good laws. Striking sections of the book are concerned with the problems attending various kinds of usurpation or attempted usurpation – the case of the tyrant who wishes to destroy the liberties of a state, that of a general who wishes to overthrow a jealous prince, that of a reformer who wishes to make changes which the people may not welcome, that of the conqueror who intends to enlarge the frontiers of his state, that of the citizen who under the disguise of beneficence and humanity is really aiming at the acquisition of power. There is the chapter already mentioned on Conspiracies. And a surprisingly large section of the book is concerned with questions relating to the art of war.

Machiavelli, then, consciously or unconsciously, exercised an important process of selection in his development of a science of statecraft. What purports to be the wisdom of the ancients is the wisdom which Machiavelli's eye seized upon and his mind chose to take. The political world that might be constructed from his books would closely resemble that of Renaissance Italy. It might be argued that the immense importance which he attached to the art of war, the emphasis which he placed upon the personal military capacity of princes, and the attention which he paid to the military aspect of governmental activity were the result of his admiration and study of republican Rome. These things represented the point at which he regarded his contemporaries as most open to criticism; they represent perhaps the most important lesson which he drew for contemporary rulers from ancient history. It is possible also to say that Machiavelli's interest as a historian and as a student of classical writers on history and politics, led to special preoccupation with the origin of states, the processes they undergo, the crises they have to pass through, and the cataclysms to which they are subject; and this might help to account for the emergency character of so much of his statecraft and that tendency in him to concern himself with issues of a violent nature.

POLITICAL SCIENTIST OR OPPORTUNIST?

Science and Political Theory

ERNST CASSIRER

Ernst Cassirer (1874–1945) is a respected name in the fields of philosophy and political science. From 1905 until 1941 he taught at the Universities of Berlin, Hamburg, Göteborg, and Oxford. In 1941 he came to the United States, where he taught at Yale until 1944 and then at Columbia before his death in 1945. Cassirer's published works are very penetrating, and include such books as *The Philosophy of Symbolic Forms*, 3 vols. (1923–29), which has been one of the major contributions to modern philosophy; *Individuum und Kosmos in der Philosophie der Renaissance* (1927); *The Philosophy of the Enlightenment* (1932. English edition in 1951); *The Platonic Renaissance in England* (1932, and 1954); and *An Essay on Man* (1944).

THE MACHIAVELLI LEGEND

Since the times of Herder and Hegel we have been told that it is a mistake to regard Machiavelli's *Prince* as a systematic book — as a *theory* of politics. Machiavelli, it is said, never meant to offer such a theory; he wrote for a special purpose and for a small circle of readers. "The *Prince*," says L. Arthur Burd in the introduction to his edition of Machiavelli's work, "was never meant except for Italians, and Italians too of a given period; indeed, we may go further and ask whether it was ever intended even for all Italians." But is there any evidence that this current opinion is a correct expression of Machiavelli's own views and of his principal purpose? Had Machiavelli no other interest, and no other ambition, than to act as a spokesman of Italy, and were all his counsels restricted to a special moment in Italian history? Was he convinced that these views were not applicable to the political life and problems of future generations?

I am unable to find a single conclusive proof of this thesis. I fear lest we are suffering from a sort of political illusion when judging in this way. We are liable to a mistake that may be called "the historian's fallacy." We are lending our own conception of history and historical method to an author to whom these conceptions were entirely unknown and to whom they would have been hardly understandable. To us it seems to be quite natural to envisage everything in its own surroundings. We consider this maxim to be a sort of categorical imperative for every sound interpretation of human actions and the phenomena of culture. Accordingly we have developed a feeling about the individuality of things and the relativity of judgments that often makes us oversensitive. We hardly dare to make a general statement; we mistrust all clear-cut formulae; we are skeptical of the possibility of eternal truths and universal values. But this was not the attitude of Machiavelli nor was it that of the Renaissance. The artists, the scientists, the philosophers of the Renaissance did not know of

From Ernst Cassirer, *The Myth of the State* (Garden City: Doubleday Anchor, 1955), pp. 154–60, 177–80, 190–94. Reprinted by permission of the Yale University Press.

our modern historical relativism; they still believed in an absolute beauty and an absolute truth.

In the case of Machiavelli himself there was a further and special reason that would forbid all those restrictions of his political theory which have been introduced by his modern commentators. He was a great historian; but his conception of the task of history was widely different from ours. He was interested in the statics not in the dynamics of historical life. He was not concerned with the particular features of a given historical epoch but sought for the recurrent features, for those things that are the same at all times. Our way of speaking of history is individualistic; Machiavelli's way was universalistic. We think that history never repeats itself; he thinks that it always repeats itself. "Anyone comparing the present with the past," he says,

will soon perceive that in all cities and in all nations there prevail the same desires and passions as always have prevailed; for which reason it should be an easy matter for him who carefully examines past events, to foresee those which are about to happen in any republic, and to apply such remedies as the ancients have used in like cases. . . . But these lessons being neglected or not understood by readers, or if understood by them, being unknown to rulers, it follows that the same disorders are common to all times.

He who would forecast what is about to happen should, therefore, always look to what has been; for all human events, whether present or to come, have their exact counterpart in the past. "And this, because these events are brought about by men, whose passions and dispositions remaining in all ages the same, naturally give rise to the same effects."

It follows from this static view of human history that all historical events are interchangeable. Physically they have a definite place in space and time; but their meaning and their character remain invariable. Now the thinker who could expound his own political maxims and theories in a commentary on the work of Titus Livy certainly

did not share the conception of our modern historians that every epoch is to be measured by its own standards. To him all men and all ages were on the same level. Machiavelli does not make the slightest distinction between the examples taken from the history of Greece or Rome and those taken from contemporary history. He speaks in the same tone of Alexander the Great and Cesare Borgia, of Hannibal and Lodovico il Moro. In the same chapter in which he deals with the "new principalities" of the Renaissance he speaks of Moses, Cyrus, Romulus, Theseus. Even Machiavelli's own contemporaries, the great historians of the Renaissance, noticed and criticized this defect of his method; Guicciardini especially made very interesting and pertinent remarks to this point.

If a thinker of this type undertook to build up a new constructive theory, a real science of politics, he certainly could not mean to restrict this science to special cases. However paradoxical it may sound, we must say that in this case our own modern historical sense has blinded us and prevented us from seeing the plain historical truth. Machiavelli wrote not for Italy nor even for his own epoch, but for the world — and the world listened to him. He would never have agreed at all with the judgment of his modern critics. What they praised in him would have been regarded by him as a defect. He looked upon his political work as Thucydides did upon his historical work. He saw in it a $\kappa\tau\hat{\eta}\mu\alpha$ $\dot{\epsilon}s$ $\dot{\alpha}\epsilon\acute{\iota}$, an everlasting possession, not an ephemeral thing. Machiavelli was, in fact, overconfident in all his judgments. He was very fond of the boldest generalizations. From a few examples taken from ancient or modern history, he immediately drew the most far-reaching conclusions. This deductive way of thinking and arguing must always be taken into consideration if we are to understand the results of Machiavelli's theory. It was not his intention to describe his own personal experiences or to speak to a special public. Of course he made use of his own experience. In the dedication of his *Discourses* he tells his friends, Zanobi Buondelmonte and Cosimo Ruccellai, that the work which he offers to them contains all the political knowledge that he had collected from much reading and long experience in the affairs of the world. Yet Machiavelli's rather scanty experience of the affairs of the world would never have enabled him to write a work of the stature and importance of *The Prince*. For this quite different intellectual powers were needed, the power of logical deduction and analysis and that of a really comprehensive mind.

There is still another prejudice that has prevented many modern writers from seeing Machiavelli's *Prince* in its true light. Most of these writers, if not all of them, began with a study of Machiavelli's life. Here they hoped to find the clue to his theory of politics. It was taken for granted that a full knowledge of the *man* Machiavelli was enough to give us a full insight into the meaning of his work. Thanks to modern biographical research the Machiavelli of former times, the "murderous" Machiavelli of the Elizabethan drama has completely disappeared. We see Machiavelli as he really was, as an honest and upright man, a fervent patriot, a conscientious servant of his country, a loyal friend, and a man devoted to his wife and children. Yet if we read all these personal qualities into his book we are mistaken. We fail to see both its fundamental merits and defects. It is not only the hypertrophy of our historical but also that of our psychological interest that has often confused our judgment. Former generations were interested in a book itself and studied its contents; we begin with psychoanalyzing its author. Instead of analyzing and criticizing Machiavelli's *thoughts* most of our modern commentators only ask for his *motives*. An amazing effort has been made to clear these motives; the question has become one of the most warmly debated in the whole literature on the subject.

I do not intend to go into the details of this discussion. The question of motives is always a difficult and precarious one — only

in a few cases can it be decided with absolute certainty. But even if we could answer it in a clear and satisfactory way, that would not help us very much. The motives of a book, and the purpose for which it was written, are not the book itself. They are only the occasional cause; they do not make us understand its systematic purport. Earlier times suffered from a certain lack of biographical material; we perhaps suffer from the very contrary. We have read Machiavelli's intimate letters; we have studied his political career in every detail; we have read not only *The Prince* but all his other writings. But when it comes to the decisive point of judging *The Prince* both in its systematic meaning and its historical influence we are at a loss. Many modern students of Machiavelli are so very much absorbed in the particulars of his life that they begin to lose a grip on the whole; they do not see the wood for the trees. In order to save the reputation of the author they minimize the importance of his work. "What was there in the *Prince*," asks a recent biographer,

to occasion so much feeling and controversy? . . . The answer to the query now as it always has been in reality is — *Nothing*. There is nothing in the *Prince* to justify the hatred, the contempt, the loathing and horror that it called forth, just as there is nothing in it to merit the praise awarded by its enthusiasts who have read into it an interpretation of their own deeds and ideals. The prince himself, the procedure he is recommended to follow, the aims he is taught to keep in view, are all products of the age, and the counsel offered by Machiavelli is that which experience had taught him to regard as the best one for the times — the only one likely to be understood and respected in that era.

If this judgment were true the whole fame of Machiavelli would, to a large degree, be due to a mistake. Not Machiavelli himself, but his readers created his fame, and they could only do so by entirely misunderstanding the sense of his work.

That seems to me to be a very poor escape from the dilemma. The dilemma really exists. There seems to be a flagrant contradiction between Machiavelli's political doctrine and his personal and moral character. But we must certainly seek for a better explanation of the problem than to deny the originality or the universality of Machiavelli's theory. If this interpretation were right, we could of course, still regard Machiavelli as a great publicist and as the spokesman and propagandist for special political and national interests. Yet we could not see in him the founder of a new science of politics — the great constructive thinker whose conceptions and theories revolutionized the modern world and shook the social order to its foundations. . . .

THE MORAL PROBLEM IN MACHIAVELLI

We need not enter here into a discussion of the vexed problem whether the last chapter of *The Prince,* the famous exhortation to deliver Italy out of the bonds of barbarians, is an integral part of the book or a later addition. Many modern students of Machiavelli have spoken of *The Prince* as if the whole book were nothing but a preparation for this closing chapter, as if this chapter were not only the climax but also the quintessence of Machiavelli's political thought. I think this view to be erroneous, and, as far as I see, the *onus probandi* rests in this case with the advocates of the thesis. For there are obvious differences between the book taken as a whole and the last chapter, differences of thought and differences of style. In the book itself Machiavelli speaks with an entirely detached mind. Everyone may hear him and make what use he will of his advice which is available not only to the Italians but also to the most dangerous enemies of Italy. In the third chapter Machiavelli discusses at great length all the errors committed by Louis XII in his invasion of Italy. Without these errors, he declares, Louis XII would have had no difficulty in attaining his end, which was to subjugate the whole of Italy. In his analysis of political actions Machiavelli never gives vent to any personal feelings of sympathy or antipathy. To put it in the words of Spinoza he

speaks of these things as if they were lines, planes, or solids. He did not attack the principles of morality; but he could find no use for these principles when engrossed in problems of political life. Machiavelli looked at political combats as if they were a game of chess. He had studied the rules of the game very thoroughly. But he had not the slightest intention of changing or criticizing these rules. His political experience had taught him that the political game never had been played without fraud, deception, treachery, and felony. He neither blamed nor recommended these things. His only concern was to find the best move — the move that wins the game. When a chess champion engages in a bold combination, or when he tries to deceive his partner by all sorts of ruses and stratagems, we are delighted and admire his skill. That was exactly Machiavelli's attitude when he looked upon the shifting scenes of the great political drama that was played before his eyes. He was not only deeply interested; he was fascinated. He could not help giving his opinion. Sometimes he shook his head at a bad move; sometimes he burst out with admiration and applause. It never occurred to him to ask by whom the game was played. The players may be aristocrats or republicans, barbarians or Italians, legitimate princes or usurpers. Obviously that makes no difference for the man who is interested in the game itself — and in nothing but the game. In his theory Machiavelli is apt to forget that the political game is not played with chessmen, but with real men, with human beings of flesh and blood; and that the weal and woe of these beings is at stake.

It is true that in the last chapter his cool and detached attitude gives way to an entirely new note. Machiavelli suddenly shakes off the burden of his logical method. His style is no longer analytical but rhetorical. Not without reason has that last chapter been compared to Isocrates' exhortation to Philip. Personally we may prefer the emotional note of the last chapter to the cold and indifferent note of the rest of the book. Yet it would be wrong to assume that in the book Machiavelli has concealed his thoughts; that what is said there was only a sham. Machiavelli's book was sincere and honest; but it was dictated by his conception of the meaning and task of a *theory* of politics. Such a theory must describe and analyze; it cannot blame or praise.

No one has ever doubted the patriotism of Machiavelli. But we should not confuse the philosopher with the patriot. *The Prince* was the work of a political thinker — and of a very radical thinker. Many modern scholars are liable to forget or, at least, to underrate this radicalism of Machiavelli's theory. In their efforts to purge his name from all blame they have obscured his work. They have portrayed a harmless and innocuous but at the same time a rather trivial Machiavelli. The real Machiavelli was much more dangerous — dangerous in his thoughts, not in his character. To mitigate his theory means to falsify it. The picture of a mild or lukewarm Machiavelli is not a true historical portrait. It is a "fable convenue" just as much opposed to the historical truth as the conception of the "diabolic" Machiavelli. The man himself was loath to compromise. In his judgments about political actions he warned over and over again against irresolution and hesitation. It was the greatness and the glory of Rome that in Roman political life all half measures were avoided. Only weak states are always dubious in their resolves, and tardy resolves are always hateful. It is true that men, in general, seldom know how to be wholly good or wholly bad. Yet it is precisely this point in which the real politician, the great statesman, differs from the average man. He will not shrink from such crimes as are stamped with an inherent greatness. He may perform many good actions, but when circumstances require a different course he will be "splendidly wicked." Here we hear the voice of the real Machiavelli, not of the conventional one. And even if it were true that all the advice of Machiavelli was destined only for the "common good," who is the judge of

this common good? Obviously no one but the prince himself. And he will always be likely to identify it with his private interest: he will act according to the maxim: *L'état c'est moi.* Moreover, if the common good could justify all those things that are recommended in Machiavelli's book, if it could be used as an excuse for fraud and deception, felony, and cruelty, it would hardly be distinguishable from the common evil. . . .

THE TECHNIQUE OF POLITICS

Yet if *The Prince* is anything but a moral or pedagogical treatise, it does not follow that, for this reason, it is an immoral book. Both judgments are equally wrong. *The Prince* is neither a moral nor an immoral book; it is simply a technical book. In a technical book we do not seek rules of ethical conduct, of good and evil. It is enough if we are told what is useful or useless. Every word in *The Prince* must be read and interpreted in this way. The book contains no moral prescripts for the ruler nor does it invite him to commit crimes and villainies. It is especially concerned with and destined for the "new principalities." It tries to give them all the advice necessary for protecting themselves from all danger. These dangers are obviously much greater than those which threaten the ordinary states — the ecclesiastic principalities or the hereditary monarchies. In order to avoid them the ruler must take recourse to extraordinary means. But it is too late to seek for remedies after the evil has already attacked the body politic. Machiavelli likes to compare the art of the politician with that of a skilled physician. Medical art contains three parts: a diagnosis is the most important task. The principal thing is to recognize the illness at the right moment in order to be able to make provision against its consequences. If this attempt fails the case becomes hopeless. "The physicians," says Machiavelli,

say of hectic fevers, that it is no hard task to get the better of them in their beginning, but difficult to discover them: yet in course of time, when they have not been properly treated and distinguished, they are easily discovered, but difficult to be subdued. So it happens in political bodies; for when the evils and disturbances that may probably arise in any government are foreseen, which yet can only be done by a sagacious and provident man, it is easy to ward them off; but if they are suffered to sprout up and grow to such a height that their malignity is obvious to every one, there is seldom any remedy to be found of sufficient efficacy to repress them.

All the advice of Machiavelli is to be interpreted in this spirit. He foresees the possible dangers that threaten the different forms of government and provides for them. He tells the ruler what he has to do in order to establish and to maintain his power, to avoid inner discords, to foresee and prevent conspiracies. All these counsels are "hypothetical imperatives," or to put it in the words of Kant, "imperatives of skill." "Here," says Kant, "there is no question whether the end is rational and good, but only what one must do in order to attain it. The precepts for the physician to make his patient thoroughly healthy, and for a poisoner to ensure certain death, are of equal value in this respect, that each serves to effect its purpose perfectly." These words describe exactly the attitude and method of Machiavelli. He never blames or praises political actions; he simply gives a descriptive analysis of them — in the same way in which a physician describes the symptoms of a certain illness. In such an analysis we are only concerned with the truth of the description, not with the things spoken of. Even of the worst things a correct and excellent description can be given. Machiavelli studied political actions in the same way as a chemist studies chemical reactions. Assuredly a chemist who prepares in his laboratory a strong poison is not responsible for its effects. In the hands of a skilled physician the poison may save the life of a man — in the hands of a murderer it may kill. In both cases we cannot praise or blame the chemist. He has done enough if he has taught us all the processes that are required for preparing the poison and if he has given us its chemical formula. Machiavelli's *Prince* contains many dangerous and poisonous things, but he looks at them with the coolness and indifference of a scientist. He gives his political prescriptions. By whom these prescriptions will be used and whether they will be used for a good or evil purpose is no concern of his.

What Machiavelli wished to introduce was not only a new science but a new *art* of politics. He was the first modern author who spoke of the "art of the state." It is true that the idea of such an art was very old. But Machiavelli gave to this old idea an entirely new interpretation. From the times of Plato all great political thinkers had emphasized that politics cannot be regarded as mere routine work. There must be definite rules to guide our political actions; there must be an art (*technē*) of politics. In his dialogue *Gorgias* Plato opposed his own theory of the state to the views of the sophists — of Protagoras, Prodikos, Gorgias. These men, he declared, have given us many rules for our political conduct. But all these rules have no philosophical purport and value because they fail to see the principal point. They are abstracted from special cases and concerned with particular purposes. They lack the essential character of a technē — the character of universality. Here we grasp the essential and ineradicable difference between Plato's technē and Machiavelli's *arte dello Stato*. Plato's technē is not "art" in Machiavelli's sense; it is knowledge (*epistēmē*) based on universal principles. These principles are not only theoretical but practical, not only logical but ethical. Without an insight into these principles no one can be a true statesman. A man may think himself to be an expert in all problems of political life, because he has, by long experience, formed right opinions about political things. But this does not make him a real ruler;

and it does not enable him to give a firm judgment, because he has no "understanding of the cause."

Plato and his followers had tried to give a theory of the *Legal* State; Machiavelli was the first to introduce a theory that suppressed or minimized this specific feature. His art of politics was destined and equally fit for the illegal and for the legal state. The sun of his political wisdom shines upon both legitimate princes and usurpers or tyrants, or just and unjust rulers. He gave his counsel in affairs of state to all of them, liberally and profusely. We need not blame him for this attitude. If we wish to compress *The Prince* into a short formula we could perhaps do no better than to point to the words of a great historian of the nine-teenth century. In the introduction to his *History of English Literature* Hippolyte Taine declares that the historian should speak of human actions in the same way as a chemist speaks of different chemical compounds. Vice and virtue are products like vitriol or sugar and we should deal with them in the same cool and detached scientific spirit. That was exactly the method of Machiavelli. To be sure he had his personal feelings, his political ideals, his national aspirations. But he did not allow these things to affect his political judgment. His judgment was that of a scientist and a technician of political life. If we read *The Prince* otherwise, if we regard it as the work of a political propagandist, we lose the gist of the whole matter.

Machiavelli the Scientist

LEONARDO OLSCHKI

Leonardo Olschki was born in Verona, Italy, in 1885. His higher education was completed at Heidelberg, where he received his Ph.D. in 1908. He became a lecturer and then professor at Heidelberg from 1909 until 1932, and taught as a visiting professor at Rome and at Johns Hopkins University in Baltimore. From 1944 until quite recently he was at the University of California. Olschki's *The Genius of Italy,* published in 1949, is a stimulating examination of Italian life, thought, and politics, both past and present.

THE profit Machiavelli gained from these imaginary conversations [with the ancients through the study of history] he collected mainly in his treatise on the prince. According to the same letter to Vettori, its purpose was to debate "what a principate is, what the species are, how they are gained, how they are kept, and how they are lost." This is, in all evidence, an essentially scientific approach to the problem at hand. In this formulation it does not involve practical questions, utilitarian interests or technical details. In Machiavelli's own description of his work the problem appears in a strictly theoretical isolation and limitation. The discussion aims at a definition of the political phenomenon and at the classification of its different aspects. The author considers only the modes and circumstances of the historical and political process in order to explain how events come to pass. He excludes from the first every debate on causes, finality, and the reasons "why." The treatise itself realizes these intentions mainly in the first part, which is almost exclusively devoted to statements and judgments of a more rigorous theoretical nature.

The scientific character of *The Prince* has been always noticed and many times emphasized, but never correctly described and accurately disclosed. In most of those cases the term "science" has been vaguely and abusively employed in order to signify the rational character of Machiavelli's thought and the objectivity of its literary expression. In that sense the term is a mere metaphor for the designation of an intellectual trend and style but no precise characterization of a body of theoretical knowledge acquired through systematic investigation, logical reasoning, and methodical procedure. It is our task to establish whether his political rationalism is truly and consistently scientific, and consequently in harmony with the intentions expressed in his letter to Vettori.

The different interpretations given his work and doctrines seem to speak against this assumption. But these contradictory appreciations of the intimate structure of Machiavelli's work and thought may also depend upon the many emotional, practical, and literary interferences which frequently trouble and alter the original logical scheme. These aspects of *The Prince* are no less captivating, remarkable, and Machiavellian. But it is only by putting aside temporarily the patriotic, personal, erudite, and pragmatic aspects of his treatise that it may be possible to catch and describe the logical procedure which led to the development of his philosophy.

From Leonardo Olschki, *Machiavelli the Scientist,* (Berkeley: The Gillick Press, 1945), pp. 22–33. Reprinted by permission of the author.

Machiavelli took the first step in this direction when he decided to consider the historical process in itself, in the way described in his letter. Through this limitation of his task the interpretation of history and of political action found itself almost automatically emancipated from all metaphysical, moral, and pious implications as well as from merely literary idealization and scholarly concerns. Man as a "civic animal" appeared to Machiavelli in the same pagan and profane, but not godless, isolation in which he was already used to contemplate human accomplishments in the light of humanism and antiquity. The idea of Divine Grace and Providence disappeared as a leading and determining force in political destinies and historical events only to be replaced by human nature, political skill, and armed power as decisive factors of the historical process. Considered in this secular sphere, antiquity and reality seem to coincide. He did not need to reject metaphysics, ethics, theology, and idealism. Ancient history showed man acting as his own master and on his own account and behalf. It disclosed politics as it always was and always will be.

By asking how principalities are won, how they are held or lost, Machiavelli transformed history into an empirical science and made of politics a system of universal rules. This complete secularization and activation of history converted the moderate rationalism of the humanist scholars and theorists into a general interpretation of the structure and development of states. By his initial attitude toward that problem and its clear general formulation Machiavelli created a "scienza nuova" in the same way Galileo started, at the end of the century, his new science of motion and a new natural philosophy; that is, by circumscribing the phenomena in their own sphere and field as independent objects of a methodical interpretation. When Galileo set himself — in 1590 — to discover not *why* things fall but *how,* natural science found itself separate from all the metaphysical, ontological, and moral implications with which it had been connected as a part of a comprehensive system of knowledge.

In both their cases the two great Florentines felt that the first condition for a direct insight into the true nature of the phenomena — human or natural — consisted in disentangling the problems from the traditional habits of thought in which they had been enmeshed and rooted for many centuries. The first attempt in that direction had been undertaken in Machiavelli's immediate neighborhood and in different fields of scientific investigation by his contemporary fellow-countryman, Leonardo da Vinci. The great artist's studio and workshop was situated next to the palace where the Florentine secretary had his office for almost fourteen years. In 1502 both met at the court of Cesare Borgia, and soon after that they collaborated in the attempted regulation of the lower course of the Arno River near Pisa.

Machiavelli strove to gain a theoretical insight into the intricacies of history and politics just as Leonardo passionately endeavored to transform the art of painting and the craft of engineering into a coherent body of scientific and empirical cognitions. In doing so the two great men first proclaimed their dissociation from the mere literary and erudite representatives respectively of political and historical and scientific or technological theories. Machiavelli asserts that, in discussing the methods and conduct of a prince, he "breaks away completely from the principles laid down by *his* predecessors." Likewise Leonardo emphatically scoffed at the "pigritia et comoditate de'libri" and at "the vaunters and declaimers of the others," and frankly proclaimed that "though he may not, like them, be able to quote other authors, he'll rely on experience, the mistress of their masters."

In both cases the direct theoretical approach to the realities of life and nature typifies the creative ardor which opened new horizons to science and history. It is characteristic of the men who absorbed the whole culture of their epoch without bending to the rules and habits of faculties and schoolmen. None of them, and none of the leading spirits of the Renaissance went through a regular curriculum of the contemporary schools and universities. They grew up as free men in a world so deeply permeated by a revived secular civilization that the heritage from antiquity became an inseparable aspect of their contemporary world. It was only in this way that the two Florentines came to contemplate Man and Nature, that is, human and natural history, "in proprio loco," independently of metaphysical and teleological connections.

On this basis they became convinced that political as well as natural phenomena are ruled by intrinsic laws to be discovered by an inductive method of thinking. Leonardo decided to put forward, as he said, "in the course of his work of science, any *general rule* derived from a previous conclusion." Machiavelli used the same words and procedure in disclosing an infallible "regola generale" also in historical events and political developments. In the writings of these two Florentines the same terms and concepts appear at the same epoch and in the same intellectual environment as original expressions of a new approach to the basic problems of science and history.

The essential difference between Machiavelli and Leonardo consists in the fact that the great artist never was able to find a common principle for the coordination of the prodigious variety of phenomena he studied, collected, observed, described, and reproduced in countless rudimentary and complicated experiments. The deep tragedy of this great man consists in his inability to discover a principle of order for the heterogeneous knowledge he had accumulated in decades of intense investigations. Therefore he could never attain a "regola generale" in any field of science. Because of this lack of a theoretical foundation all his persistent attempts to solve the basic problems of mechanics could only produce the chaotic multitude of scattered and contradictory fragments into which his work had necessarily disintegrated. There is no "regola generale" in his science of motion, which ignored some basic theoretical presupposition indispensable for the formulation of natural laws.

As paradoxical as it may appear, Machiavelli had a more consistent and refined scientific instinct than Leonardo because his whole philosophy was based on axiomatic assumptions which made his system of thoughts and facts possible and consistent. He believed that human nature was always and everywhere the same, and that the real sense of history can be understood because — in his own words — men, just as heaven, the sun, and the elements, never had changed their motion, order, and power. This almost naturalistic concept of man and his destinies may logically imply the negation of history, but practically it represents the foundation of the whole Machiavellian doctrine of the eternal recurrence of typical events and of the possible renewal of culminating historical situations through voluntary imitation of typical political accomplishments.

The axiom that human nature is constant has its exact scientific counterpart in Galileo's fundamental assumption that "matter is unalterable, i.e., always the same, and that because of its eternal and necessary character it is possible to produce demonstrations of it no less straight and neat than those of mathematics." Galileo's interpretation of natural phenomena stands on this assumption, which includes the philosophical justification of experimental science and confirms his idea of the physical unity of the universe. Without their general statements neither of the two great Florentines could have achieved the elaborate systems of doctrines which inaugurated a new era of human thought. No law of nature, no "regola generale" of history could be formulated, or even conceived, without a theoretical assumption of a universal value.

Certainly, the idea that human nature is immutable had already been expressed by some philosophers of antiquity, and the ubiquitous and inalterable character of matter had been taught, with different interpretations and conclusions, by the Greek atomists, Aristotle and the Averroistic school. But in no case did those concepts inaugurate and determine a rational system of doctrine. The basic axioms of Machiavelli's political theories and of Galileo's natural philosophy are so deeply embodied in their thought and experiences that both their systems stand or fall with the acceptance or rejection of their respective fundamental principles.

We may debate about Galileo's concept of matter, which is no more accepted in the way he had it in mind. Machiavelli's views of the constancy of human nature can be admitted only in the psychological field. It cannot be extended to the mutable intellectual sphere. However it may be, the two basic axioms have lost nothing of their philosophical purport and scientific importance. It is because of their elementary evidence that Galileo's achievements are still fundamental in spite of our new insight into the structure of matter and many changes in the basic physical concepts. Likewise Machiavelli's doctrines have not lost anything of their actual and universal interest after so many changes in political science and in the structure of human society.

The Myth of Machiavelli's Political Science

JOSEPH KRAFT

Joseph Kraft is a highly successful free-lance writer and analyst of foreign affairs. In 1951 he was at the Institute for Advanced Study at Princeton, where he wrote the following article, later becoming an editorial writer for *The Washington Post*. For six years he was a regular contributor to the Sunday *New York Times* "News of the Week in Review." Kraft's articles have appeared in such varied publications as *Harper's, Esquire, The Saturday Evening Post, The New Leader, The Observer* of London, and *L'Express* of Paris. In 1958 he won the Overseas Press Club award for the best magazine reporting of foreign affairs.

In an oft-quoted sentence, Robert von Mohl writes, "Machiavelli has sinned, but he has been even more sinned against." And without assessing the respective burdens of guilt, it is clear that the second proposition of Mohl's epigram is valid — Machiavelli has been slandered. It is also clear that most anti-Machiavellian criticism, however sincere, partakes of a common error. Machiavelli, to be specific, has been abstracted from sixteenth-century Florence and has been made responsible for Henry VIII, Frederick the Great, Adolf Hitler, or whoever the reigning tyrant may be. But whereas such unhistorical procedure has been effectively denounced by Machiavelli's supporters, these supporters have indulged themselves in the same fancy with impunity, thereby sinning against Machiavelli out of the purest affection. James Burnham, for instance, after correctly insisting that, in respect to Adolf Hitler, Machiavelli died in 1527, prolongs Machiavelli's life in respect to more admirable figures and asserts that Machiavelli "shared the methods of science with Galileo and Darwin and Einstein." Nor is Burnham unique. Both Max Lerner and Pasquale Villari, Machiavelli's scholarly biographer, share Burnham's predilections. They, too, make a distinction between the unpleasant world of scientific truth, the world of hard, cold facts, and the rosy, poetical world of fancies and ideals. And they, too, deeming it a service, place Machiavelli, with his eyes open to harsh reality, in this cold world of facts. Accordingly, Burnham's statements that Machiavelli attempted an "accurate and systematic description of public facts" and that "there are no dreams or ghosts in Machiavelli. He lives and writes in a daylight world," find echoes in Villari's observation that Machiavelli "was making a daring and gigantic effort at the investigation of the true reality of things . . . without concerning himself with individual judgments or prejudices." And this motion is seconded by Max Lerner, who declares that "*The prince* . . . places itself squarely in the ranks of realism" because it is a "hard-bitten inquiry into how things actually get accomplished in a real world."

Now not only is this rigid distinction in itself dangerous, if not wholly unreal, but there is also prima facie evidence that, if it is applied to Machiavelli, he should not be placed in the camp of the realists. To make such a disposition would be to take Machiavelli too much at his own word. For, cheek by jowl with Machiavelli's claims that he

From Joseph Kraft, "Truth and Poetry in Machiavelli," *Journal of Modern History*, XXII (1951), 109–10, 116–21. Reprinted by permission of the author and the University of Chicago Press.

describes the world as it actually is, there are remarks that clearly indicate that Machiavelli's "daylight world" was by no means ghostless and that Machiavelli was rather extravagant with the method of "Galileo and Darwin and Einstein." I refer, of course, to Machiavelli's little-noted remarks about the world of spirits, prodigies, and portents. In the last chapter of *The prince*, Machiavelli speaks of these occult matters in dead earnestness, informing Lorenzo de Medici that the time is propitious for action because "unexampled wonders have been seen here performed by God, the sea has been opened, a cloud has shown you the road, the rock has given forth water, manna has rained." And, lest it be thought that this was a play to Lorenzo's superstitious imagination, it should be noted that in *The Discourses* Machiavelli devotes a whole chapter to "prove that no great events ever occur in any city or country that have not been predicted by soothsayers, revelations, or by portents and celestial signs." Furthermore, not content with merely stating this *fact*, Machiavelli borrows the ingenious explanation "that the air is peopled with spirits, who by their superior knowledge foresee future events, and out of pity for mankind warn them by such signs, so that they may prepare against the coming evils." Thus Machiavelli looks upon the systematic collection of supernatural information as a part of political science and not as a romantic belief remote from the world of action. Indeed, it is recorded that upon the capture of Pisa in June 1509 Machiavelli, who was in touch with Florentine astrologers, postponed the occupation of Pisa to a more favorable day and hour.

This evidence, to be sure, is hardly momentous. It does, however, rather take the edge off a comparison between Machiavelli and Darwin, and it effectively serves to put Machiavelli where he belongs, in the ghostly world of sixteenth-century Florence. Nevertheless, it would be absurd to conclude that Machiavelli was a mystic suffering from hallucinations. The test of science is the reasonableness of the discov-

ery, not the credulousness of the discoverer. And in this respect the case for Machiavelli as scientist is still good. . . .

But [still] not so clean and neat, to return to our original argument, is the contention that Machiavelli, a dispassionate observer of the facts, is the Darwin of politics. Rather this contention is messy with black marks. Machiavelli did not observe the facts closely. His deductions were, in many cases, illogical. He utterly misread the general military picture of the day. He rejected the newest weapons and stipulated for the oldest. And, finally, face to face with the uncongenial facts of military life, he displays tender inhibitions and delicate sensibilities. The poor man appears to be as much a poet as a scientist.

Now it will be obvious that Machiavelli's consistent oversights and illogicalities cannot be explained simply by bad luck. It seems more likely, if our characterization has been accurate, that Machiavelli, along with his general want of scientific attributes, lacked also that most noble of scientific pretensions, the open mind. Something was obscuring his view and predetermining his decisions. The lush growth of error that we have just noted is rooted in the fertile field of prejudice and preconception.

One of these preconceptions, of course, has already been suggested. As Guicciardini pointed out, Machiavelli was blinded by the brilliance of Roman institutions to the developments of his own time. He could not see Gaston de Foix because his eye was fixed on Camillus. The militia was the most effective mode of fighting because it was the Roman mode. "According to the authority of the Romans and the example of ancient armies we should value infantry more than cavalry." According to the authority of the Romans we should discount artillery, it is only another form of the military elephant. According to the example of ancient armies we should neglect firearms, they are only another form of the scythed chariot. And so Machiavelli goes, page after page, approving only that which was "anciently used" and giving no consideration to the intrinsic merits of the things he disapproved. Antiquity became in Machiavelli's hands an infallible ruler, an absolute standard of good and bad. As a result, it also became a source of systematic error.

Moreover, at the risk of being tedious, it must be pointed out that Machiavelli's reverence for Roman antiquity, though it partakes of the humanistic spirit, is also in part quite independent. Machiavelli's mistakes, in other words, cannot be wholly excused by those of his contemporaries. Leonardo da Vinci and Leon Battista Alberti both admired the antique, but both warned against a too literal imitation; and Alberti pointedly dedicated his treatise on painting to Filippo Brunelleschi. For Machiavelli, however, ancient Rome was more than a potential source of inspiration; it was a weapon with which he could beat his contemporaries. Moreover, granted Machiavelli's theory of history, the grandeur that was Rome was a logical necessity. One might almost say that had there been no Rome, Machiavelli would have had to invent one.

Machiavelli's concept of history presupposes a Rome because for Machiavelli the process of history is one of corruption and decay from original pristine purity. Thus: "Those are the best constituted bodies, and have the longest existence, which possess the intrinsic means of frequently renewing themselves, or such as obtain this renovation in consequence of some extrinsic accidents. And it is a truth clearer than light, without such renovation, these bodies cannot continue to exist; *and the means of renewing them is to bring them back to their original principles.*"[1] Accordingly, Machiavelli praises the French *parlement* which, so he thinks, perpetually returns France to her original principles, thus preventing the normal accretion of corruption.

To be sure, it may fairly be argued that Machiavelli's statements imply only that history is cyclical and not that it is in perpetual decay. According to this view, there

would be as much chance for growth as for decay. And it must, in this connection, be admitted that in the *Discourses* Machiavelli indisputably pays the homage of imitation to Polybius' cyclical theory of political development. But even here the accent is on decay. Furthermore, the argument that Machiavelli conceives history cyclically is more substantial in theory than in application. For it may be set down as a general rule that there is something disingenuous about most cyclical theorists. Almost invariably they place *themselves* in a period of decline — in the sewer of centuries, at the *fin de siècle,* or on the fringe of the advancing lava. It even seems that the whole fabric of cyclical theory has been woven only to cloak an opinion of contemporary corruption and chaos. Apart from any question of universal validity, however, this generalization applies to Machiavelli. He marks no growth. Certain countries, notably Switzerland and Germany, have not fallen as far from the ancient peak as others. But as to Italy, time and again Machiavelli denounces its corruption. He observes in *The Art of War* that "our discipline is now depraved." Elsewhere in the same book, Machiavelli charges that the Italians "live a lazy indolent life free from trouble and inconvenience," and this fact, he asserts, is "the cause of our degeneracy and the present neglect of military discipline." But the want of military discipline is only one manifestation of Italian corruption. Luxury, ambition, and faction (lack of patriotism) are other elements of Italian degeneracy. Thus the luxury at the papal court has destroyed all piety in Italy. Thus, too, Machiavelli's militia ordinance of 1512 goes to fantastic lengths to repress faction and ambition. The ancient Romans, on the other hand, are commended because in Rome, so Machiavelli alleges, there was no seeking after office and because these Romans had laws that kept their citizens poor. In this very chapter, as a matter of fact, Machiavelli, on the grounds "that this subject has been so often illustrated by other writers," disdains to demonstrate that

---

[1] Author's italics.

"poverty produces better fruits than riches — that the first has conferred honor upon cities, countries, and religions whilst the latter have served only to ruin them." For Machiavelli, therefore, sixteenth-century Italy, rich with commercial profits, is actually quite degenerate. Her men are weak and ambitious, her governments corrupt and divided.

Now there is no quarrel with Machiavelli's estimate of his fellow-Italians. Probably he is very close to the truth. Our appeal, however, is based not on the decision but on the trial. What constitutes Machiavelli's prejudice is his theory of history. For the theory disqualifies him from being a competent judge of what was going on around him. If the course of history is decay and if the only cure is renovation, a return to first principles, then innovation is a delusion and progress a lie. The fortress and the siege gun, like the development of a money economy, serve only to enervate mankind. Anything new is perforce bad. It weans us from our "ancient wisdom and austere control." Machiavelli, having drawn his curve, extrapolates from it. But this trick, useful in calculus, is fatal in history. In history each point is a little independent of its predecessors, and the deviation is crucial.

It may fairly be concluded, then, that Machiavelli's reverence for ancient Rome, coupled with his concept of history, involved him in two preconceptions, two commitments that disqualify him from the role of a cool, detached observer: first, he was led to advocate an almost slavish copying of Roman institutions, and, second, he was unable to calculate correctly the influence of material progress. One of the most pregnant forces in all history completely escaped his notice.

In addition, as a footnote to this discussion, it must be explicitly declared that Machiavelli's preconceptions are fundamentally antiscientific. In science the advancement of knowledge — and it is no accident that the phrase is Bacon's — proceeds not by renovation, not by an ever-

lasting return to Galen, but incrementally, by the unceasing addition of new observations and generalizations. Thus it is no exaggeration to say with a modern writer, "Admiration of the ancients and submission to their authority had to go, before science could find a place in the sun."

Science, of course, has found its place. But before we can find a conclusion one more point must be considered. It is the tricky and trying subject of Machiavelli's psychology. What is it, according to Machiavelli, that keeps the ball of human affairs rolling? Or, to use Lerner's handy phrase, how are "things actually accomplished in a real world?"

The first thing to notice is Machiavelli's theory of the uniformity of humanity. "In all his works," writes Villari, "not only political and historical, but likewise literary, Machiavelli reiterates a thousand times, both in prose and verse, that men are always the same, that their nature knows no change, and that the same accidents are perpetually repeated in the world." Villari is not overstating the case. To the point of tedium, Machiavelli repeats his formula: "All men are born and live and die in the same way, and therefore resemble each other." Occasionally he explains himself, declaring that "all cities and all peoples are and ever have been animated by the same desires and the same passions." But in essence his message is constant: all men, in all places, at all times, are similar because they all want the same things.

Now such a statement implies a good deal. It denies, first of all, that experience — what happens to us — is unique and personal. More important, it asserts in a subtle manner that experience is inconsequential. For, if the root of our sameness is the similarity of our passions and if, through thick and thin, these remain fundamentally unchanged, it follows that the thick and the thin are of secondary importance. What happens to us, then, is of little moment, that hard core of passions and desires, the will, is perfectly constant. Men are but bathers in the sea of experience; upon their death they emerge from the sea as they entered it, quite naked. The tides wash all about, but if they occasionally displace the bather, they do not affect his insides, his motivating nucleus.

What this means is that, for Machiavelli, man the bather is essentially disembodied will. As his militia ordinance fully testifies, Machiavelli believes that man can will anything; his ambitions are boundless, his passions endless, his guile bottomless. He can act the part of a lion and then, quickly changing his mind, play the fox. He can murder and appear to be gentle; sin and pretend religion. Each part can be lightly cast off as dead skin. For experience has no direction or force. It does not control man. It does not focus conscience or force his will. Man, in short, can will what he wills.

No doubt these considerations will seem remote from our original line. They are not. For Machiavelli's psychology, also, involves a preconception. Here, too, is an opinion not based on minute observation, an opinion that distorts Machiavelli's vision and prejudices his judgments. Even fundamentally men are not all the same. For with man everything is fundamental, local custom as well as the will to power. It is not true that experience is unimportant. Man, like Tennyson's Ulysses, is a part of all that he has met. And all that he has met is no less a part of man. He is flushed to the depths of his soul by the great waves of the sea of experience. Above all, however, it is not true that man is disembodied will. The will is forced at every turn by experience. A man who has murdered is not the same. A man who has listened to the saints cannot, as Molière's Don Juan learns, pretend that he has not heard them. Experience itself has taught us this.

More to the point still, however, is the fact that this preconception is a fertile and therefore a deceptive one. Much of the best of Machiavelli follows from it. Indeed, what grows from these twisted roots constitutes Machiavelli's bid for the Darwinian mantle. For without these roots the prince

is unthinkable. The prince, too, stands outside experience. He must play a hundred parts in so detached a manner that he has no after-effects. Without believing, he must utilize the "confidence religious faith, judiciously availed of, will inspire." Without disliking him, he must kill his brother Remus. He must seem generous, and be niggardly. Occasionally he must even appear to be foolish. For "it is advisable at times to feign folly as Brutus did; and this is sufficiently done by praising, seeing, and doing things contrary to your way of thinking."

Moreover, the career as well as the technique of the prince depends upon the isolation of will. For Machiavelli believes that it is the will of the prince that gets things done. Machiavelli has no conception of an impersonal, organic development of society. Rather: "We must assume, as a general rule, that it never or rarely happens that a republic or monarchy is well constituted, or its old institutions entirely reformed, unless it is done by only one individual." As one of Machiavelli's favorite similes suggests, the prince is to his people as the sculptor is to his clay. The prince merely molds the pliant mass of his people. He shares no feelings with them, and they do not influence him. If he has steady fingers, they cannot resist his pressure, or force his hand. For the sculptor, too, in respect to his lump of clay, is disembodied will. In each case, the finished article represents only the purpose of its maker.

Now it is the creation of the role of the sculptor-prince, the legislative superman, that constitutes Machiavelli's originality. The eyes of this monster see things differently; his mind entertains a host of new ideas. First, and most important, is the idealization of the state. It is to the prince, before all men, that the state represents an ideal. The prince, more than anyone else, can believe and say: "Where the very safety of the country depends upon the resolution to be taken, no consideration of justice or injustice, humanity or cruelty, nor of glory or of shame, should be allowed to prevail. But putting all other considerations aside, the only question should be, What course will save the life and liberty of the country?"

Second, Machiavelli's most original insights into the nature of religion, justice, and war proceed from the prince. Machiavelli examines religion not as a believer but through the eyes of the prince. Thus in some cases religion is a useful fiction, for "there are many good laws, the importance of which is known to the sagacious lawgiver, but the reasons for which are not sufficiently evident to enable him to persuade others to submit to them; and therefore do wise men, for the purpose of removing this difficulty, resort to divine authority." In other cases, religion is dangerous; it withers a man's native vigor and dulls his fighting instinct. Accordingly, as if anticipating Friedrich Nietzsche, Machiavelli remarks that the principles of the Christian religion "have made men feeble, and caused them to become an easy prey to evil-minded men, who can control them more securely, seeing that the great body of men, for the sake of gaining Paradise, are more disposed to endure injuries than to avenge them."

As to justice, and political morality in general, these qualities, seen through the eyes of the prince, are not intrinsically good. At times they do keep people content, and so, judiciously applied, they are, or can be, politically useful. Conversely, as we have seen above, at times the reverse of justice is politically useful, and the prince, supposedly removed from the traditional lore of his people, will proceed accordingly with impunity. Thus war is not a moral crime. It is simply an extension of governmental policy. And "the many that are now of the opinion . . . that no two things are more discordant and incongruous than a civil and military life" are thoroughly deluded. In the politics of the prince, as in the psychology of his author, morality is not an inexplicable, and thereby undeniable, fact. It is a calculated ruse.

Here, for the first time, Machiavelli's highly vaunted freedom from prejudice

becomes apparent. It is only this last fruitful preconception that makes the Machiavelli-as-scientist claim intelligible. For Machiavelli allows nothing extraneous to interfere with the prince. Nothing is recommended on the strength of its reputation. Rather, in each case the possibilities of successful application are considered before any recommendations are made. Here is careful observation and close reasoning. It is undeniable, therefore, that Machiavelli's recommendations are useful. If we are quite sure that what we value most is the safety of the state, then there is no better man to turn to than Machiavelli. Furthermore, it is always useful to know something more about justice, religion, and war, and obviously Machiavelli has something new to say. But, as we have seen, it is equally obvious that what Machiavelli has to say is based on a controlling prepossession as to the nature of man. Machiavelli's great contribution rests, therefore, not, as some allege, on a foundation of limpid rationalism but on what amounts to a determining prejudice. A prejudice which, to be sure, allows, from one point of view, for a more rational consideration of policy, but a prejudice none the less. A prejudice which, however it may simplify political analysis, is, in the full totality of things, narrow indeed.

It is not, furthermore, a prejudice that may safely be overlooked because of its special use in political analysis. For if it is true, as seems likely, that Machiavelli is the father of modern political science, if it is true, in other words, that the modern political thinker shares Machiavelli's bias, then there is still more reason to note and make corrections for the bias. There is still more reason to deny to the Machiavellians, the strategic thinkers, and the political scientists the compulsive authority that is commonly, and perhaps unwisely, granted to natural science. For truly their authority is not intrinsically compulsive. Their science of human affairs at its inception dehumanizes the subject. It takes man out of the world of experience. It pretends that the political world is somehow different, that in the political world man, by stiffening his will, can act immorally and be the better for it. Accordingly, if these scientific pretensions are allowed, man will find himself doing in the name of science what he could never agree to in the name of mankind. If man does believe that Machiavelli's world is the cold, hard, daylight world of facts, then he will find himself casting off his morality as a poetic illusion. Thus it is in order that we state and restate that Machiavelli's work is not scientific. It is in order that we note the curiously bad results of Machiavelli's predilection for the antique, and that we stress the fact that even his most incisive thought is rooted in psychological prejudice. For should these facts escape us, Machiavelli will become more harmful than useful. The tool he has placed in our hands will turn against us, because we shall have forgotten its limitations.

Raison d'Etat in Machiavelli

FRIEDRICH MEINECKE

For more than half a century Friedrich Meinecke (1862–1954) was one of the giants of German historiography and a penetrating thinker in the field of intellectual history. For forty years, until the Nazi conquest, he was editor of Germany's leading historical journal, the *Historische Zeitschrift,* and wrote extensively on intellectual movements and problems of historiography in his *Weltbürgertum und Nationalstaat* (1908); *Die Idee der Staatsräson in der neueren Geschichte* (1924); and *Die Entstehung des Historismus,* 2 vols. (1936). As a disciple of Ranke and admirer of Goethe, Meinecke tried to combine the humanitarianism of the one and the historical objectivity of the other to produce an approach to history and politics which was both realistic and deeply philosophical.

POLYTHEISM and a secular view of human values were what nourished *raison d'état* in antiquity. At the period when the city-state was flourishing, the thing most worth living for was the State itself. The ethics of individual and of national conduct thus coincided, and so there was no conflict between politics and ethics. There was also no universal religion, to try and restrict by its commands the free exercise of State powers. The national religion which existed tended rather to favour this free exercise, by glorifying heroism. As the city-state began to dissolve, the heroic ideal passed over into the new form which power assumed in the State where men struggled fiercely, each for himself; this was the State of the ruthless man of power, classically portrayed by Plato in Callicles of the *Gorgias.* Altogether the ancient conception of *raison d'état* remained at this time firmly fixed in personalities, and served to vindicate the mode of action which was forced on contemporary rulers by pressure of the situation. It never seemed to rise (or at least not at all consistently) toward the conception of a supra-individual and independent state personality, which would stand over against the actual rulers of the time.

An epilogue and a final crushing judgment on the ancient view of *raison d'état* was given by Christianity, when Augustine said: *Remota justitia quid sunt regna nisi magna latrocinia.* The new universal religion set up at the same time a universal moral command, which even the State must obey, and turned the eyes of individual men on other-worldly values; thus all secular values, including heroism as the herald of power politics and *raison d'état,* were caused to give ground. Then in the Middle Ages Germanic jurisprudence combined with Christian ethics in keeping down the State. The State certainly existed in the Middle Ages, but it did not rank supreme. Law was set above it; it was a means for enforcing the law. "Politics and *raison d'état* were not recognized at all in the Middle Ages." Naturally, of course, the general practice was different from this theoretical view. Therefore, "since there was no place in the legal and constitutional

From Friedrich Meinecke, *Machiavellism: The Doctrine of Raison d'État and its Place in Modern History,* translated from his *Die Idee der Staatsräson in der neueren Geschichte* by Douglas Scott (New Haven: Yale University Press, 1957), pp. 26–33, 35–40, 44. By permission of the Yale University Press.

theory of mediaeval times for the demands of policy, these forced their own elemental way out."

But in the later Middle Ages these irregular outlets began to be regularized. The struggle between Church and Papacy fostered the conscious power politics of great rulers like the Emperor Frederick II and Philip IV of France. The Emperor Charles IV in Germany and King Louis XI in France were examples of a thoroughly unscrupulous and rational art of government, based on their own authority. Even the Church itself, by its inner transformations, by the progressive permeation of the Papacy with worldly political interests, by the often very utilitarian approach of the Church Councils, and by the rational perfecting of Papal finance, paved the way for a new spirit in the art of incipient growth of national States, and in the struggles of the more important dynasties, whose possessions had been amassed by feudal methods, to safeguard these possessions by nonfeudal means, by adhesive methods of government. The universal ideas of this mediaeval *corpus christianum* moved continuously toward a new centre of Will concentrated in the State. . . .

Nevertheless the modern Western world has inherited one legacy of extraordinary importance from the Christian and Germanic Middle Ages. It has inherited a sharper and more painful sense of the conflict between *raison d'état* on the one hand, and ethics and law on the other; and also the feeling which is constantly being aroused, that ruthless *raison d'état* is really sinful, a sin against God and divine standards, a sin against the sanctity and inviolability of the law of the good old times. The ancient world was already familiar with these sins of *raison d'état*, and did not omit to criticize them, but without taking them very much to heart. The very secularity of human values in the ancient world made it possible to view *raison d'état* with a certain calmness and to consider it the outcome of natural forces which were not to be subdued. Sinfulness in antiquity was

still a perfectly naïve sinfulness, not yet disquieted and frightened by the gulf between heaven and hell which was to be opened up by Christianity. This dualistic picture of the world, which was held by dogmatic Christianity, has had a deep influence even on the period of a Christianity that is growing undogmatic; and it has given the problem of *raison d'état* this deeply felt overtone of tragedy, which it never carried in antiquity.

It was therefore a historical necessity that the man, with whom the history of the idea of *raison d'état* in the modern Western world begins and from whom Machiavellism takes its name, had to be a heathen; he had to be a man to whom the fear of hell was unknown, and who on the contrary could set about his life-work of analyzing the essence of *raison d'état* with all the naïvety of the ancient world.

Niccolò Machiavelli was the first to do this. We are concerned here with the thing itself, not with the name for it, which he still did not possess. Machiavelli had not yet compressed his thoughts on *raison d'état* into a single slogan. Fond as he was of forceful and meaningful catch-words (coining many himself), he did not always feel the need to express in words the supreme ideas which filled him; if, that is, the thing itself seemed to him self-evident, if it filled him completely. For example, critics have noticed that he fails to express any opinion about the real final purpose of the State, and they have mistakenly deduced from this that he did not reflect on the subject. But, as we shall soon see, his whole life was bound up with a definite supreme purpose of the State. And in the same way his whole political way of thought is nothing else but a continual process of thinking about *raison d'état*.

Machiavelli's system of thought was brought into being by an absolutely special and sublime, and at the same time extraordinary, conjunction of events: the coinciding of a political collapse with a spiritual and intellectual renaissance. In the fifteenth century Italy enjoyed national independence, and was, in the pregnant words of Machiavelli (*Principe*, ch. 20), *in un certo modo bilanciata* by the system of five States which kept each other within bounds: Naples, the Papal States, Florence, Milan, and Venice. There was growing up in Italy, fostered by all the realistic elements in Renaissance culture and directly promoted by the arrangement (which was just coming into fashion) of having permanent embassies, a form of statecraft which was carried on according to fixed and definite rules. This statecraft culminated in the principle of *divide et impera,* it taught that everything ought to be considered with a view to its usefulness, it surmounted all religious and moral limitations in a naïvely playful manner, but itself functioned by means of relatively simple and mechanical operations and thought-processes. Only the catastrophes which overtook Italy after 1494, with the invasion by the French and the Spanish, the decline of Neapolitan and Milanese independence, the precipitate change in the form of government in Florence, and most of all the collective impact of foreign countries on the entire Apennine peninsula — only these catastrophes succeeded in maturing the spirit of politics to that point of passionate strength, depth and acuteness, which is revealed in Machiavelli. As a secretary and diplomat of the Florentine Republic until the year 1512, he learnt everything that Italian statecraft had achieved up to that time, and he was also beginning already to shape his own original thoughts on the subject. What caused them to pour out suddenly after 1512 was the crushing fate which overtook both him and the republic in that year. As a member of the party which had been overthrown and was being temporarily persecuted, Machiavelli, in order to re-establish himself, was forced to seek the favour of the new rulers, the Medicis, who were once more in power. Thus a conflict arose between his own personal and egotistical interests, and the ideals of republican freedom and the city-state which he had held up to now. It is indeed the greatness of Machiavelli that he strove

now to settle this conflict, and bring it to a final issue. Against the obscure and not particularly attractive background of his own naïve and unscrupulous egoism, there came into being the new and masterly reflections on the relation between republic and monarchy, and about a new national mission of monarchy; it was in a context of all this that the whole essence of *raison d'état,* compounded of mingled ingredients both pure and impure, both lofty and hateful, achieved a ruthless expression. He had reached his fortieth year — the age at which productive scientific minds often give of their best — when after 1513 he wrote the little books about the prince and the *Discorsi sopra la prima deca di Tito Livio.* . . .

In spite of his outward respect for the Church and for Christianity (frequently mingled with irony and criticism), and in spite of the undeniable influence which the Christian view had on him, Machiavelli was at heart a heathen, who levelled at Christianity the familiar and serious reproach (*Disc.*, II, 2) of having made men humble, unmanly, and feeble. With a romantic longing he gazed toward the strength, grandeur, and beauty of life in antiquity, and toward the ideals of its *mondana gloria.* He wanted to bring back once again that united strength of sense and intellect in the natural genuine man, where *grandezza dell'animo* and *fortezza del corpo* combined together to create heroism. He broke then, with the dualistic and one-sidedly spiritualizing ethic of Christianity, which depreciated the natural impulses of the senses. Although indeed he retained some of its structural ideas about the difference between good and evil, he strove principally for a new naturalistic ethic which would follow the dictates of nature impartially and resolutely. For whoever follows these dictates (as he said once) can find no fault in carrying on lighthearted amorous affairs in the midst of serious business — even Nature is full of change and contradiction.

This kind of naturalism can easily lead to a harmless and unreflecting multiplicity in the question of human values. But (in spite of the offering which he gladly brought to the altar of Venus) Machiavelli concentrated all his real and supreme values in what he called *virtù*. This concept is exceedingly rich in meaning, and although it was taken over from the tradition of antiquity and humanism, it had been felt and elaborated in a quiet individual manner; ethical qualities were certainly embraced in it, but it was fundamentally intended to portray something dynamic, which Nature had implanted in Man — heroism and the strength for great political and warlike achievements, and first and foremost, perhaps, strength for the founding and preservation of flourishing States, particularly republics. For in the republics, of which Rome in its great republican period seemed to him an ideal example, he saw the conditions most favourable for the generation of *virtù*. It therefore embraced the civic virtues and those of the ruling class; it embraced a readiness to devote oneself to the common good, as well as the wisdom, energy, and ambition of the great founders and rulers of States. But the *virtù* which the founder and ruler of a State had to possess counted for Machiavelli as *virtù* of a higher order. For in his opinion this kind of *virtù* was able, by means of appropriate "regulations," to distil out of the thoroughly bad and wretched material of average specimens of humanity the other kind of *virtù* in the sense of civic virtue; to a certain extent the latter was *virtù* of a secondary quality, and could only be durable if it was rooted in a people whose spirit was naturally fresh and unspoilt. This separation of *virtù* into two types, one original and the other derived, is of exceptional significance for a complete understanding of the political aims of Machiavelli. For it shows that he was a long way from believing uncritically in the natural and imperishable virtue of a republican citizen, and that he viewed even the republic more from above, from the standpoint of the rulers, than from underneath, from the standpoint of broad-based democracy. . . . Thus his

concept of *virtù* formed a close link between republican and monarchial tendencies, and, after the collapse of the Florentine Republic, enabled him without inconsistency to set his hopes on the rule of the Medicis, and to write for them the Book of the Prince. In the same way it made it possible for him immediately afterwards to take up again in the *Discorsi* the strain of republicanism, and to weigh republic and monarchy against one another.

Moreover, his own special ethic of *virtù* — a product of the joyous worldly spirit of the Renaissance — begins now to throw light on the relation in which he stands to the ordinary Christian, and so-called genuine, morality; this relationship has been the cause of much dispute and a continual subject of reproof to Machiavelli. We have already remarked that he retained the basic Christian views on the difference between good and evil. When he advocated evil actions, he never denied them the epithet "evil" or attempted any hypocritical concealment. Nor did he dare to embody direct traits of morally wicked behaviour in his ideal of *virtù*. In Chapter 8 of the *Principe*, which deals with Agathocles, he says that to murder one's co-citizens, to betray one's friends, to be lacking in loyalty, piety, and religion, cannot deserve the name of *virtù*; these things can achieve mastery, but not glory. And yet in Agathocles, who behaved in this way, he recognized at the same time a real *virtù* and *grandezza dell'animo*, i.e. great virtues of a ruler. The ethical sphere of his *virtù* therefore lay in juxtaposition to the usual moral sphere like a kind of world of its own; but for him it was the higher world, because it was the vital source of the State, of the *vivere politico*, the supreme task of human creativity. And because it was for him the higher world, so it could be permitted to trespass and encroach on the moral world in order to achieve its aims. . . .

The most serious discrepancy in his system of thought — a discrepancy which he never succeeded in eliminating and which he never even tried to eliminate — lay between the newly discovered ethical sphere of *virtù,* and of the State animated by *virtù,* on the one hand, and the old sphere of religion and morality on the other. This *virtù* of Machiavelli was originally a natural and dynamic idea, which (not altogether unhappily) contained a certain quality of barbarity (*ferocia*); he now considered that it ought not to remain a mere unregulated natural force (which would have been in accordance with the spirit of the Renaissance) but that it ought to be raised into a *virtù ordinata,* into a rationally and purposively directed code of values for rulers and citizens. The *virtù ordinata* naturally set a high value on religion and morality, on account of the influence they exerted toward maintaining the State. In particular, Machiavelli spoke out very forcibly on the subject of the indispensability of religion (*Disc.,* I, 11 and 12); at any rate, he was strongly in favour of a religion which would make men courageous and proud. He once named "religion, laws, military affairs" together in one breath, as the three fundamental pillars of the State. But, in the process, religion and morality fell from the status of intrinsic values, and became nothing more than means toward the goal of a State animated by *virtù.* It was this that led him on to make the double-edged recommendation, which resounded so fearsomely down the centuries to come, inciting statesmen to an irreligious and at the same time dishonest scepticism: the advice that even a religion tinged with error and reception ought to be supported, and the wiser one was, the more one would do it (*Disc.,* I, 12). Whoever thought like this was, from a religious point of view, completely adrift. What final certainty and sure foundation was there left in life, if even an unbelieved and false religion could count as valuable, and when moral goodness was seen as being a product of fear and custom? In this godless world of Nature man was left alone with only himself and the powers Nature had given him, to carry on the fight against all the fateful forces wielded by this same Nature. And

this was exactly what Machiavelli conceived his own situation to be.

It is striking and forceful to observe how he strove to rise superior to it. On the one side *fortuna,* on the other *virtù* — this was how he interpeted it. Many people today (he says in ch. 25 of the *Principe*), in the face of the various blows of Fate and unsuspected revolutions we have experienced, are now of the opinion that all wisdom is entirely unavailing against the action of Fate, and that we must just let it do what it likes with us. He admits that even he himself has occasionally felt like this, when in a gloomy mood. But he considered it would be lacking in *virtù* to surrender to the feeling. One must rouse oneself and build canals and dams against the torrent of Fate, and then one will be able to keep it within bounds. Only half our actions are governed by Fortune; the other half, or almost half, is left to us. "Where men have not much *virtù,* then *fortuna* shows its strength clearly enough. And because it is full of change, so there are numerous changes in republics and states. And these will always go on changing, until sooner or later there will come a man who so loves antiquity, that he will regulate *fortuna;* then it will not be able to show every twenty-four hours how much it is capable of accomplishing" (*Disc.,* II, 30). *Fortuna* has got to be beaten and bruised like a woman one wants to possess, and boldness and barbarity will always be more successful there than coldness. But this boldness has got to be united with great cunning and calculation, for each situation of fate demands a method specially suited for dealing with it. He began to meditate very deeply on just this particular problem, for it showed up very clearly both the powers and the limitations of *virtù* and of humanity altogether. The individual agent cannot escape the nature he is born with. He acts in such and such a way because this nature requires it. Hence it arises that, according to the disposition of Fate, this same method which his character dictates will turn out well one day, and badly the next (*Disc.,*

III, 9). An insight of this kind could lead back to fatalism. But the effect on him of all these doubts and impulses was like the bending of a taut-strung bow. He let fly his arrows with all the more force.

Enemies learn to use each other's weapons. *Virtù* has the task of forcing back *fortuna*. *Fortuna* is malicious, so *virtù* must also be malicious, when there is no other way open. This expresses quite plainly the real spiritual origin of Machiavellism: the infamous doctrine that, in national behaviour, even unclean methods are justified, when it is a question of winning or of keeping the power which is necessary for the State. It is the picture of Man, stripped of all transcendent good qualities, left alone on the battlefield to face the daemonic forces of Nature, who now feels himself possessed too of a daemonic natural strength and returns blow for blow. In Machiavelli's opinion, *virtù* had a perfectly genuine right to take up any weapon, for the purpose of mastering Fortune. One can easily see that this doctrine, which appeared so dualistic on the outside, had really sprung from the background of a naïve Monism, which made all the powers of life into forces of Nature. It now became a presupposition for the discovery which Machiavelli had made about the essence of *raison d'état*.

But in order to make this discovery, yet another theory was needed — one which he thought out and applied just as clearly and consistently as he did the theory of the struggle between *virtù* and *fortuna*. This was the theory of *necessità*. *Virtù, fortuna,* and *necessità* are three words which keep on sounding again and again throughout his writings with a kind of brazen ring. These words, and perhaps also the refrain of the *armi proprie* (which sums up the demands he made on the State in the way of military matters and power politics), show his ability to condense the wealth of his experience and thought, and how the rich edifice of his mind rested on a few quite simple but solid pillars. For him *virtù* and *necessità* were related in a way very similar to that in which, in modern philos-

ophy, the sphere of values is related to the sphere of causal connection; i.e. where the causal connection provides the means and possibility of realizing the values. If *virtù* was the vital power of men, a power which created and maintained States, and gave them the sense of meaning, then *necessità* was the causal pressure, the means of bringing the sluggish masses into the form required by *virtù*. . . . The more *necessità* there is, he insists in the *Discorsi*, I, 1, the more *virtù* there will be also, and *necessità* can bring us to many things, which reason is not strong enough to drive us to (*Disc.*, I, 1). And alongside the conception of *virtù ordinata* he placed the equally characteristic conception of *necessità ordinata dalle leggi* (*Disc.*, I, 1) as engendering first-class human material for the State. Thus it is always a question of following the natural forces of life, but also at the same time of regulating them by means of reason. If one were to adopt for a moment the unlovely nomenclature of "isms," one could call his system a trial of naturalism, voluntarism, and rationalism. But without his belief (rooted in universal history) in the positive *blessing* of *necessità*, without the real warmth which he gave it, he would never have come to proclaim with such determination and conviction that which one can call the *curse* of *necessità*, of necessity of State.

One more trait of his personality must have contributed: namely, the quite unconventional and at the same time radical nature of his thought, which never shrank back before any abyss. Certainly his contemporaries too had long learnt never to shrink back before any moral abyss, and to wade quite cheerfully through any filth. For if it had not been for the general stultifying of moral feeling in life, and without examples offered by the Papacy from the time of Sixtus IV and Alexander VI, with his frightful son Cesar Borgia, Machiavelli would never have had the milieu required for his new ideas about the use of immoral methods in politics. They were indeed not new as regards content; but they were new in the sense that he dared to express them, and to combine them into a system which embraced a universal outlook. For up till now theory had only limped after practice. The selfsame humanists who, like Pontanus at the court of Naples, saw clearly all the dark side of the new statecraft, were indeed prepared to permit cunning and deception when it was for the good of the community; but after that they fell back once more on the formal pattern of the figure of the Prince, filled in with classic phrases. If I am to offer something really useful, says Machiavelli, it seems to me more suitable to follow the real truth of things, rather than the imaginary picture one has of them. Many people have imagined for themselves republics and principalities, the like of which one has never seen or even thought possible for the difference between what one actually does and what one ought to do is so great that whoever, in considering how people ought to live, omits to consider how they behave, is riding for a fall. That is to say, the man who makes it a rule in all circumstances to perform nothing but good actions, is bound to go under amongst so many who are evil. Therefore it is "necessary" for a prince, if he is to maintain his position, to learn also how not to be good, and then to utilize or not utilize this knowledge, as *necessità* prescribes.

It is worthy of notice that Machiavelli did not introduce near the beginning of his essay on the Prince this new principle of method — a principle which was to break fresh ground for so many centuries and which was so purely empirical and so completely free from presuppositions. He does not bring it in till much further on, in Chapter 15. For he himself underwent development, during the course of his work on the book. Chapter 15 belongs (as we have tried to prove elsewhere), not to the original conception of the *Principe,* but rather to an extension of it which probably came soon afterwards. Henceforth he always exercised the new principle, which was closely akin to the aesthetic honesty and directness of Florentine art. Then,

when he was in the full spate of work, he suddenly became conscious that he was treading new paths. It was the climax of his life, and at the same time also a turning point for the history of European thought. And in this matter history of thought touched very closely upon the history of nations; they were both struck by the *same* electric shock. Even if the statesmen themselves learnt nothing new from it, the very fact that it was *being taught* was still new. For it was not until after it had been grasped as a principle, that the historical tendencies achieved their full power of impact, and reached the stage when they could be called ideas.

But the initial application of the new scientific method, and its effect on historical life, were frightful and shattering. A prince must also learn how not to be good —this was the requirement of *necessità,* by which all human life was governed and constrained. But it was quite another matter to decide whether, on the one hand, the moral law should be broken only in the practice of politics, or whether, on the other hand, it was permissible to justify (as from now on became possible, and in fact more and more tended to happen) such an infringement by the plea of an unavoidable "necessity." In the first instance the moral law itself had, in its sanctity as a supra-empirical necessity, remained entirely unimpaired. But now this supra-empirical necessity was broken down by an empirical necessity; the force of evil was fighting for a place alongside that of good, and was making out that it was, if not an actual power of good, then at least an indispensable means for obtaining a certain kind of goodness. The forces of sin, which had been basically subdued by the Christian ethic, now won what was fundamentally a partial victory; the devil forced his way into the kingdom of God. There now began that dualism under which modern culture has to suffer: that opposition between supra-empirical and empirical, between absolute and relative standards of value. It was now possible for the modern State, following its own inmost vital impulse, to free itself from all the spiritual fetters that had constrained it; it was possible for it, as an independent power acknowledging no authority outside this world, to effect the admirable accomplishments of rational organization, which would have been unthinkable in the Middle Ages, but were now due to increase from century to century. But it already contained the poison of an inner contradiction, from the very moment it began its ascent. On the one hand religion, morality, and law were all absolutely indispensable to it as a foundation for its existence; on the other hand, it started off with the definite intention of injuring these whenever the needs of national self-preservation would require it. But surely (it would be asked) Machiavelli must have felt this contradiction, and the serious consequences it was bound to have?

He was not able to feel it, for the reason that his cast-iron theory of *necessità* concealed it from him, or because (as he believed, at least) the theory of *necessità* resolved the contradiction. The same force which impelled princes to refrain from being good under certain circumstances, also impelled men to behave morally; for it is only from necessity that men perform good actions. (*Principe*, ch. 23). Necessity was therefore the spear which at the same time both wounded and healed. It was the causal mechanism which, provided that *virtù* existed in the State, saw to it that the necessary morality and religion were present, and that any failings in that respect were made good. Thus the theory of the struggle between *virtù* and *fortuna*, and the

theory of *necessità*, worked together very closely to justify the prince in the use of underhand measures and to prevent this from being harmful to his opinion. . . .

All this shows that he moved on the ethical heights of a *raison d'état* which within the limits of his time could only have limited aims indeed, but which was capable of a vital consciousness of the good of the community, the *bene comune* of the whole people. And ultimately he was even capable of rising to the highest ethical feeling which is possible for action prompted by *raison d'état;* this sacrifice consists in taking on oneself personal disgrace and shame, if only it offers a means of saving the Fatherland. Occasionally he would express it in the very same breath with his prosaic utilitarianism: "It will always be difficult to win the masses over to such conclusions as these, which appear to indicate cowardice and defeat, but do in reality signify salvation and gain" (*Disc.,* I, 53). But the heights and depths of his *raison d'état* are united in the most powerful manner by that phrase, which is to be found at the end of his *Discorsi* (III, 41), and which must surely have sounded in the ears of a certain great German statesman during the First World War: that one may save the Fatherland even *con ignominia.* "When it is a question of saving the Fatherland, one should not stop for a moment to consider whether something is lawful or unlawful, gentle or cruel, laudable or shameful; but, putting aside every other consideration, one ought to follow out to the end whatever resolve will save the life of the State and preserve its freedom."

Politics and Morals

GEORGE PEABODY GOOCH

Few modern scholars have had such a long, productive, and varied career as has the distinguished British historian G. P. Gooch. Born in 1873 and trained at London, Cambridge, Berlin, and Paris, Gooch embarked on a life of unceasing activity and accomplishment, which included four years as a member of Parliament, president of the Historical Association, president of the National Peace Council, president of the English Goethe Society, editor of *Contemporary Review,* and joint editor of *The Cambridge History of British Foreign Policy* and *British Documents on the Origins of the War.* The list of Gooch's published works is long and impressive. He has been particularly productive and distinguished in the areas of modern English, French, and German history, nineteenth-century historiography, and modern diplomatic history.

Four hundred years ago Machiavelli proclaimed the divorce of politics from morals in a little book which is still very much alive. Numberless rulers in all times and countries had anticipated in practice the advice which he gave in *The Prince,* but the thought of the Middle Ages ran on transcendental lines. Its publicists strove to deduce the maxims of statecraft from the teachings of the Old and New Testaments, and even the worst monarchs paid lip-service to the Christian creed. By contemptuously brushing aside all religious and ethical considerations, and approaching the problem of government in a spirit of naked realism, the audacious Florentine thinker, far more than Columbus or Copernicus, Erasmus, or Luther, ushered in the modern world. For the dominating intellectual feature of the last four centuries, as Lecky pointed out long ago, is the secularization of thought. The spell of authority had been broken before Machiavelli sat down to write; but it required a thoroughgoing pagan to preach the gospel of pure empiricism and to turn his back on the ideas of a thousand years. It is true enough that he was primarily concerned with the fortunes of Italy, distracted as she was by the torments of invasion and civil strife; and his book closes with an appeal to the House of Medici. In *The Prince,* however, as with Burke's *Reflections on the French Revolution,* it is not the chronological setting but the conception of the nature of man and society that matters to us today. It is one of the merits of Machiavelli, and one of the sources of his enduring influence, that he says precisely what he thinks.

Let us recall some of his familiar maxims, set forth in the level tones with which a clinical lecturer explains the nature and maladies of the human frame. "He who neglects what is done to follow what ought to be done will sooner learn how to ruin than how to preserve himself. For a tender man and one that desires to be honest in everything must needs run a great hazard among so many of a contrary principle. Wherefore it is necessary for a prince to harden himself and learn to be good or otherwise according to the exigence of his affairs. For if we consider things impartially we shall find some things in appearance are virtuous, and yet, if pursued, would bring certain destruction; and others, on the contrary, that are seemingly bad, which, if followed by a prince, procure his

From G. P. Gooch, *Studies in Diplomacy and Statecraft* (New York: Longmans, Green & Co., 1942), pp. 311–13, 316, 319–22. Reprinted by permission of the publishers.

peace and security." "Is it better to be be-
loved than feared, or to be feared than be-
loved? Both would be convenient, but
because that is hard to attain, it is better
and more secure to be feared." "How honourable it is for a prince to keep his word
everybody understands. Nevertheless experience has shown in our times that those
who have not tied themselves to it have
done great things, and by their cunning
and subtlety have overcome those who have
been superstitiously exact. For you must
understand that there are two ways of con-
tending, by law and by force. The first is
proper to men, the second to beasts. But
because many times the first is insufficient,
recourse must be had to the second. It belongs therefore to a prince to understand
both. Seeing therefore it is of such importance to take upon him the nature and disposition of a beast, of all the whole flock
he ought to imitate the lion and the fox.
A prince who is wise and prudent cannot
or ought not to keep his word when the
keeping of it is to his prejudice, and the
causes for which he promised or removed.
Were men all good this doctrine should not
be taught; but because they are wicked and
not likely to be punctual with you, you are
not obliged to any such strictness with
them."

Here is the sinister gospel in its crudest
form of what the French call *raison d'état,*
the doctrine that extraordinary objects cannot be achieved under the ordinary rules,
and that the monarch, in seeking the welfare of the state as he understands it, is
fettered by no human or divine laws. This
is not to say that might is right or that the
end, whatever it be, justifies the means; for
the exercise of power has to be related to
the single definite purpose of the interest
of the state. The supreme qualification for
the ruler in the eyes of Machiavelli and
his disciples is *virtù,* which means not virtue but virility, energy, force of character,
remorseless vigour, the head to plan and the
arm to strike. The paramount duty of the
representative and guardian of the community is to survive and succeed. For this
purpose he must circumvent and intimidate

his enemies at home and abroad. Half
measures, hesitation, weakness of will and
purpose, are the supreme offence. Hence
the fascination exerted by Caesar Borgia on
the Florentine Secretary and diplomatist,
who knew him in the flesh. On the other
hand the author of *The Prince* has as little
use for the brutal and blundering tyrant as
for the ineffectual idealist. To make ome-
lettes you must break eggs, but there is no
excuse for breaking them if you cannot
prepare a tasty dish. Intelligence is at least
as necessary as resolution. The prince must
be worthy of his post, and must win acceptance from his subjects if not their love.
"Better than any number of fortresses is not
to be hated by your people." His whole
duty is to save, to strengthen, and to maintain the state.

Whether the ship is steered by a hereditary monarch or a dictator, an aristocracy,
a parliament, or a committee of public
safety, is irrelevant. Machiavelli is primarily interested, not in the forms of government, but in the way it is carried on. Gov-
ernance is a problem of strength and skill,
not of ethics and law. A régime must be
judged, not by intentions, but by the fruits
of its policy. Of such notions as the *Respublica Christiana,* the unity of civilization,
allegiance to humanity, joint responsibility
for the welfare of the world, there is not a
trace. *Virtù, Fortuna, Necessità:* here was
the new trinity which Machiavelli substi-
tuted for the Christian creeds. Each political unit, large or small, must think solely
of itself. The morals of the jungle are exalted into a philosophy of life. Anticipating
Nietzsche he complains that Christianity is
the religion of the weak. The author of
The Prince was certainly no worse a man
than his contemporaries in the courts and
cabinets of the Renaissance, and indeed he
modelled his technique on the experiences
of his own career. But the horror with
which plain citizens heard of his counsels
is suggested by the fact that "Old Nick,"
though already a familiar *alias* for the devil,
came to be associated with his name; that
The Prince was called the Devil's Cate-
chism or the Ten Commandments Reversed;

that the adjective "Machiavellian" is still in use all over the world to denote the stratagems of statecraft at its worst. That he denounced bad rulers in his larger work, the *Discourses on Livy,* and confessed that the practice of breaking the laws for good ends lent a colour to breaches committed for bad ends, has been overlooked. It is by *The Prince* that he stands or falls. . . .

The enduring vitality of *The Prince* cannot be airily dismissed as a regrettable token of human depravity. Its teaching has been watered down in the course of the centuries, but a sediment of the Florentine gospel is left in numberless thinkers of the last four centuries who bear a better name. In Acton's learned Introduction to Burd's edition of *The Prince,* and in Meinecke's massive treatise *Die Idee der Staatsräson,* we are confronted with a serried array of authorities, some of them of high repute, who, while rejecting the grosser features of the system, argue that public and private morals are not and can never be quite the same; that supreme emergencies call for exceptional methods; that Machiavelli is useful as medicine though indigestible if consumed as our daily bread. We recall Cavour's revealing cry of distress while he was putting Italy on the map: "What rascals we should be if we did for ourselves what we do for our country!" However lofty our political ideals, however firm our moral principles, we cannot shirk the rude challenge of *The Prince.* Can rulers, must rulers, invariably attempt to apply the moral law, as the private citizen in civilized communities is rightly expected to do? Or is the art of government, to borrow a phrase of Nietzsche, beyond good and evil? . . .

Is the outlook really so hopeless, the problem really so insoluble, as these teachers suggest? That the struggle between Kratos and Ethos will continue indefinitely we can readily believe. But may not the relations of the combatants change? May not Ethos extend its sway at the cost of Kratos, even if it cannot hope for victory all along the line? Does not the history of man illustrate the slow advance of moral principle, the occupation of one piece of territory after another previously claimed without challenge by the rival principle of force? May not this process be continued almost indefinitely as pioneers rescue the desert and the forest for the haunts of men, and engineers turn the shallow waters into fertile land?

Our answer to these questions will depend in the main on our view of human nature. The differences in the systems of political philosophy throughout the ages reflect still deeper divergences in our interpretation of man. If we believe, like Machiavelli and Hobbes, that he is nearer to the beasts than to the angels, we shall lean to the doctrines of autocracy and the sovereign state. It is equally natural that those who take a more favourable view should contest the universal supremacy of force, and should preach the gospel of partnership and cooperation on every plane. "Man," declared Humboldt, "is naturally more disposed to beneficent than to selfish actions." Everyone knows Kant's famous confession of his ever-increasing wonder at the starry heavens above and the moral law within. The conviction that society rests on moral and spiritual foundations was shared by Burke, the greatest of English political thinkers, who described the state as a partnership in all art, in all science, in all perfection. And Mill based the most moving plea for individual liberty ever written on his lofty reading of the character and potentialities of man. Democracy is more than a type of government, and what is called pacifism is more than a mere theory of international relations. Both are the expression of faith in the ultimate sanity of the common man, in his power to learn from experience, in his capacity for spiritual growth.

I share this faith. Despite the number and the eminence of his disciples, I believe that Machiavelli is unfair to mankind. The professed realist only saw a limited portion of the vast field of experience. The will to power is not the sole key to human nature. History is assuredly a record of strife — the strife of arms and wits; but it is also, as Kropotkin reminded us in an illuminating work, a story of mutual aid. Noble aims in plenty have been formed by men and nations, and many of them have been wholly or partially achieved. With a longer and a wider experience than Machiavelli, we have learned to recognize the solid core of truth in the old adage that honesty is the best policy. The application of the maxims of *The Prince* may achieve a temporary triumph, but they provide no foundation for the enduring happiness, prosperity, or security of a state. If man were indeed the unruly and perfidious animal that he believes, *The Prince* might be accepted as a recipe for making the best of a bad job. But the broad testimony of modern history suggests that the average man rises above this level. Our sixteenth-century instructor makes no allowance for growth; the idea of progress is the creation of modern times, above all of the eighteenth century. Froude used to say that history is like a child's box of letters, with which you can spell any word you choose. What Machiavelli saw was real enough, and he was a careful student of history as well; but in concentrating his gaze on the practice of governments, he paid too little attention to other aspects of the life of the community. Brilliant intellects like Machiavelli and Hobbes, Voltaire and Marx have seen certain phenomena with extraordinary distinctness and emphasized their immense significance, yet vast tracts of human experience lie beyond their ken. The great Italian completely ignored the ultimate potency of moral forces. Had he been invited to forecast the future he would have predicted an essentially unchanging world. *Plus ça change, plus c'est la même chose.* His interpretation of political society was static. The human animal, as portrayed by Machiavelli, is unable to climb above the level of his baser self, as water is incapable of rising above its source.

Even those who feel themselves unable to reject his gospel outright may draw a distinction, which never occurred to the thinkers of the sixteenth century, between domestic and foreign affairs. Within the frontiers of the most civilized states responsible government has replaced autocracy, and the rule of law has superseded the whim of the ruler. For the moment there is a set-back in this process, and half Europe is in the grip of dictatorships. But I firmly believe that the liberalizing forces which have given Western civilization its peculiar stamp in the last four centuries will reassert themselves when the supermen who have challenged their validity pass away. The most satisfactory criterion of civilization is not the growth of knowledge or the increase of amenities, but the degree in which social life is humanized, individuality fostered, and political action brought within the moral sphere. In the more civilized communities the theoretical omnipotence of the executive is tempered by the fact that our rulers, like other citizens, are subject to the laws, can be sued in the courts, and can be changed by constitutional methods. With the aid of a vigilant public opinion and a free Press we have reached a stage when the government is expected not only to conform to the ordinary principles of honourable dealing but to set a shining example. . . .

It is this general acceptance today of the duty of rulers to set a good example that accounts for the world-wide horror at the murder of the Tsar and his family by the Bolshevists in 1918, and the massacre of June 30, 1934, when Hitler shot scores of his actual or potential enemies without trial. Such a swift and bloody stroke was in strict accordance with the doctrine of *The Prince* that, if the ruler strikes at all, he should hit hard and get his blow in first. But the twentieth century is not the sixteenth. When the foundations of law have been overthrown, practices long abandoned are revived by men who seize power through violence and retain it by fear. Our disgust at such reversions is a measure of the advance we have made since the times when the murder of an opponent was accepted as a matter of course.

The End of Machiavellianism

JACQUES MARITAIN

Jacques Maritain is perhaps the best-known Catholic philosopher of the mid-twentieth century. Born in 1882 and reared as a Protestant, Maritain became a Catholic in 1906 and since then has established a great reputation on both sides of the Atlantic as a liberal Neo-Thomist thinker. With a doctorate from the Sorbonne, he became a professor of philosophy at the Institut Catholique in Paris, a position he held for twenty-seven years, then at the Institut d'Etudes Médiévales in Toronto. From 1940 to 1944 he was visiting professor at Columbia and Princeton, and between 1945 and 1948 he served as French ambassador to the Vatican. Since 1948 he has been professor of philosophy at Princeton University. Maritain is the author of more than forty major books, plus numerous articles which have been published by leading scholarly journals.

IT is this common Machiavellianism that I wish now to consider. In so doing, I should like briefly to touch the three following points: first, the notion of common good and the factual triumph of Machiavellianism; second, the crucial conflict which here constitutes the main problem, and the resolution thereof; third, the roots and the more subtle implications of this resolution, which concern the specific structure of politics in its relationship with morality.

Now for my first point. For Machiavelli the end of politics is power's conquest and maintenance: which is a work of art to be performed. On the contrary, according to the nature of things, the end of politics is the common good of a united people; which end is essentially something concretely human, therefore something ethical. This common good consists of the good life — that is, a life conformable to the essential exigencies and the essential dignity of human nature, a life both morally straight and happy — of the social whole as such, of the gathered multitude, in such a way that the increasing treasure and heritage of communicable good things involved in this good life of the whole be in some way spilled over and redistributed to each individual part of the community. This common good is at once material, intellectual, and moral, and principally moral, as man himself is; it is a common good of human persons. Therefore, it is not only something useful, an ensemble of advantages and profits, it is essentially something good in itself — what the Ancients termed *bonum honestum*. Justice and civic friendship are its cement. Bad faith, perfidy, lying, cruelty, assassination, and all other procedures of this kind which may occasionally appear *useful* to the power of the ruling clique or to the prosperity of the state, are in themselves — insofar as political deeds, that is, deeds involving in some degree the common conduct — injurious to the common good and tend by themselves toward its corruption. Finally, because good life on earth is not the absolute ultimate end of man, and because the human person has a destiny superior to time, political common good involves an intrinsic though indirect reference to the absolutely ultimate

From Jacques Maritain, "The End of Machiavellianism," *The Review of Politics*, Vol. IV (Jan. 1942), pp. 9–17, 21–22, 27–28, 30–32. Reprinted by permission of the editors of the *Review of Politics*.

end of the human members of society, which is eternal life, in such a way that the political community should temporally, and from below, help each human person in his human task of conquering his final freedom and fulfilling his final destiny.

Such is the basic political concept which Machiavellianism broke down and destroyed. If the aim of politics is common good, peace — a constructive peace struggling through time toward man's emancipation from any form of enslavement — is the health of the state; and the organs of justice, above all of distributive justice, are the chief power in the state. If the aim of politics is common good, the ruler, having to take care of the temporal end of a community of human persons, and having to avoid in this task any lack of clear-sightedness and any slip of will, must learn to be, as St. Thomas taught, a man good in every respect, *bonus vir simpliciter*. If the aim of politics is power, the ruler must learn not to be good, as Machiavelli said.

The great rulers of modern times have well understood and conscientiously learned this lesson. Lord Acton was right in stating that "The authentic interpreter of Machiavelli is the whole of later history." We have to distinguish, however, two kinds of common Machiavellianism. There was a kind of more or less attenuated, dignified, conservative Machiavellianism, using injustice within "reasonable" limits, if I may put it so; in the minds of its followers, what is called *Realpolitik* was obfuscated and more or less paralyzed, either by a personal pattern or moral scruples and moral rules, which they owed to the common heritage of our civilization, or by traditions of diplomatic good form and respectability, or even, in certain instances, by lack of imagination, of boldness, and of inclination to take risks. . . .

This second form of Machiavellianism is absolute Machiavellianism. It was intellectually prepared, during the XIXth Century, by the Positivist trend of mind, which considered politics to be, not a mere art, but a mere natural science, like astronomy or chemistry, and a mere application of so-called "scientific laws" to the struggle for life of human societies — a concept much less intelligent and still more inhuman than that of Machiavelli himself. Absolute Machiavellianism was also and principally prepared by the Romanticist German philosophy of Fichte and Hegel. It is well known that Fichte made an analysis of Machiavelli part of his *Address to the German Nation:* as to the Hegelian cult of the state, it is a metaphysical sublimation of Machiavelli's principles. Now the turn has been completed, ethics itself has been swallowed up into the political denial of ethics, power and success have become supreme moral criteria, "the course of world history stands apart from virtue, blame, and justice," as Hegel put it, and at the same time "human history," he also said, "is God's judgment." Machiavellianism is no longer politics, it is metaphysics, it is a religion, a prophetical and mystical enthusiasm. . . .

Here we are confronted with that impetuous, irrational, revolutionary, wild, and demoniacal Machiavellianism, for which *boundless* injustice, *boundless* violence, *boundless* lying and immorality, are normal political means, and which draws from this very boundlessness of evil an abominable strength. And we may experience what kind of common good a power which knows perfectly how not to be good, and whose hypocrisy is a conscious and happy, ostentatious and gloriously promulgated hypocrisy, and whose cruelty wants to destroy souls as well as bodies, and whose lying is a thorough perversion of the very function of language, what kind of common good such a power is able to bring to mankind. Absolute Machiavellianism causes politics to be the art of bringing about the misfortune of men.

That's how it is. But absolute Machiavellianism succeeds, does it not? At least it has succeeded for many years. How could it not succeed, when everything has been sacrificed to the aim of success? Here is the ordeal and scandal of contemporary conscience. Moreover it would be astonishing if a timid and limited Machiavellianism were not overcome and thrown away by a boundless and cynical Machiavellianism, stopping at nothing. If there is an answer to the deadly question which we are asked by the Sphinx of history, it can only lie in a thorough reversal of a century-old political thought. In the meantime, the peoples which stand against absolute Machiavellianism will be able to stop its triumphs and to overcome its standard-bearers only in wasting and sacrificing in this struggle their blood and their wealth and their dearest treasures of peaceful civilization, and in turning against this Machiavellianism its own material weapon, material techniques, and gigantic means of destruction. But will they be obliged, in order to conquer it and to maintain themselves, to adopt not only its material weapons, but also its own spirit and philosophy? Will they yield to the temptation of losing for the sake of life their very reason for living and existing?

Here we arrive at the crucial conflict which I intend to discuss as my second point.

Confronted with any temptation of Machiavellianism, that is, of gaining success and power by means of evil, moral conscience answers and cannot keep from answering, just as when it is tempted by any profitable fault: it is never allowed to do evil for any good whatsoever. Any Christian conscience in this case is strengthened by the very word of the Gospel. When the devil tempted Jesus by showing him all the kingdoms of the world, and the glory of them, and telling him: "All these things will I give thee, if thou wilt fall down and worship me," — "Get thee hence, Satan," Jesus answered. "For it is written, Thou shalt worship the Lord thy God, and him only shalt thou serve.". . .

Yet the answer we are considering does not solve our conflict; on the contrary, it increases this conflict, it widens the tear to the infinite, it clamps down on the Machiavellian temptation without appeasing the anguish and scandal of our intellect. For it is an answer given by Personal Ethics to a question asked by Political Ethics; it transcends the state; it cuts short the question, it does not resolve it. Obviously no assertion of the individual Ethics of the Person, as absolutely true, absolutely decisive as it may be, can constitute a sufficiently adequate and relevant answer to a problem stated by the Ethics of the State. Exactly because it is a transcendent answer, it is not a proper one. Machiavellianism succeeds, does it not? Absolute Machiavellianism triumphs on earth, as our eyes have seen it for years. Is Morality willing, is Christianity willing, is God willing that, of necessity, all our freedoms be conquered, our civilization destroyed, the very hope annihilated of seeing a little justice and brotherly amity raise our earthly life — willing that, of necessity, our lives be enslaved, our temples and institutions broken down, our brethren persecuted and crushed, our children corrupted, our very souls and intelligence delivered over to perversion by the great imperial standard-bearers of Machiavellianism, because of the very fact that we adhere to justice and refuse the devil, while they dare to use injustice and evil and accede to the devil up to the end?

It is the true goal of the *Person* which is eternal, not that of the *State*. If a man suffers martyrdom and enters paradise, his own soul enjoys bliss; but suppose all the citizens of a tributary state of some Nero suffer martyrdom and enter paradise, it is not the soul of this state which will enjoy bliss; moreover, this state no longer exists. The state has no immortal soul, nor has a nation, unless perhaps as concerns a merely spiritual survival of its common moral heritage in the memory of men or in the virtues of the immortal souls which animated its members long ago, at the time when it existed. . . .

But in political life itself, in the order of nature, in the framework of the temporal laws of human existence, is it not impossible that the first of the normal means of providing the common good of a state, that is, justice and political morality, should lead to the ruin and disaster of this state? Is it not impossible that the first of the means of corrupting the common good of a state, that is, injustice and political treachery, should lead to the triumph and prosperity of this state?

Yes, this is impossible.

Yet Machiavellianism succeeds in political history? Evil succeeds?

What is then the answer?

The answer is that evil *does not* succeed. In reality Machiavellianism does not succeed. To destroy is not to succeed. Machiavellianism succeeds in bringing about the misfortune of man, which is the exact opposite of any genuinely political end. More or less bad Machiavellianists have succeeded for centuries against other more or less bad Machiavellianists, this is mere exchange of counterfeit coin. Absolute Machiavellianism succeeds against moderate or weak Machiavellianism, this also is normal. But if absolute Machiavellianism were to succeed absolutely and definitely in the world, this would simply mean that political life would have disappeared from the face of the earth, giving place to an entanglement and commixture of the life of the animals and the slaves, and of the life of the saints.

But in saying that evil and injustice do not succeed in politics, I mean a more profound philosophical truth. The endless reserves of evil, the seemingly infinite power of evil of which I spoke a moment ago, are only, in reality, the power of corruption — the squandering and dissipation of the substance and energy of Being and of Good. Such a power destroys itself in destroying that good which is its subject. The inner dialectic of the successes of evil condemn them not to be lasting. The true philosophical answer consists therefore in taking into account the dimension of time, the duration proper to the historical turns of nations and states, which considerably exceeds the duration of a man's life. According to this *political duration* of vital maturations and fructifications, I do not say that a just politics will, even in a distant future, always actually succeed, nor that Machiavellianism will, even in a distant future, always actually fail. For, with nations and states and civilizations we are in the order of nature, where mortality is natural and where life and death depend on physical as well as moral causes. I say that justice works through its own causality, toward welfare and success in the future, as a healthy sap works toward the perfect fruit, and that Machiavellianism works through its own causality for ruin and bankruptcy, as poison in the sap works for the illness and death of the tree.

Now, what is the illusion proper to Machiavellianism? It is the illusion of *immediate success*. The duration of the life of a man, or rather the duration of the activity of the prince, of the political man, circumscribes the maximum length of time required by what I call *immediate success*, for immediate success is a success that our eyes may see. But what we are speaking of, what Machiavelli is speaking of, in saying that evil and injustice succeed in politics, is in reality *immediate success,* as I defined it. Now immediate success is success for a man, it is not success for a state or a nation; it may be — it is, in the case of Machiavellianist successes considered as to their inner causal law, a disaster according to the duration proper to state-vicissitudes and nation-vicissitudes. It is with regard to immediate success that evil and injustice enjoy a seemingly infinite power: a power which can be met and overcome only by a heroical tension of the antagonistic powers. . . .

Thus it is true that politics being something intrinsically moral, the first political condition of good politics is that it be just. And it is true at the same time that justice and virtue do not, as a rule, lead us to success in this world. But the antinomy is solved, because on the one hand success in politics is not material power nor material wealth nor world-domination, but the achievement of the common good, with the conditions of material prosperity which it involves. And because, on the other hand, these very conditions of material prosperity, as terrible as the ordeals may be which the requirements of justice impose on a people, are not and cannot be put in jeopardy or to destruction by the use of justice itself, if historical duration is taken into account and if the specific effect of this use of justice is considered in itself, apart from the effect of the other factors at play. . . .

We arrive now at the third consideration I indicated at the beginning, in which I should like to make clearer certain particular points concerning the relationship between Politics and Morality.

As I have previously pointed out, political reality, though principally moral, is by essence both moral and physical, as man himself, but in a different manner from man, because it does not have any substantial immortal soul. Societies are like ever-growing organisms, immense and long-living trees, or coral-flowers, which would lead at the same time a moral and human life. And in the order to which they belong, which is that of Time and Becoming, death is natural; human communities, nations, states, and civilizations naturally die, and die for all time, as would these morally-living coral-flowers of which I just spoke. Their birth, growth, and decay, their health, their diseases, their death, depend on basic physical conditions in which the specific qualities of moral behavior are intermingled and play an essential part, but which are more primitive than these qualities. Similarly, imprudence or intemperance may hasten the death of a man, self-control may defer this death, yet in any case this man will die.

Justice and moral virtues do not prevent the natural laws of senescence of human societies. They do not prevent physical catastrophes from destroying them. In what sense are they the chief forces of the preservation and duration of societies? In the sense that they compose the very soul of society, its internal and spiritual force of life. Such a force does not secure immortality to the society, any more than my immortal soul protects me from death. Such a

force is not an immortal entelechy, because it is not substantial; yet, insofar as it is spiritual, it is by itself indestructible. Corrupt this force, and an internal principle of death is introduced into the core of the society. Maintain and improve this force, and the internal principle of life is strengthened in the society. Suppose a human community is hammered, crushed, overwhelmed by some natural calamity or some powerful enemy: as long as it still exists — if it preserves within itself justice and civic friendship and faith, there is actual hope of resurging within itself, there is a force within itself which tends by itself to make it live and get the upper hand and avail itself of disaster; because no hammer can destroy this immaterial force. If a human community loses these virtues, its internal principle of life is invaded by death.

What therefore must be said, is that justice and righteousness *tend by themselves* to the preservation of states, and to that real *success* at long range of which I spoke a moment ago. And that injustice and evil *tend by themselves* to the destruction of states, and to that real *failure* at long range of which I also spoke.

Such is the law of the fructification of human actions which is inscribed in the nature of things and which is but the natural justice of God in human history.

But if the normal fruit of success and prosperity called for by political justice and wisdom does not come into actual existence because the tree is too old or because some storm has broken its branches; or if the normal fruit of failure and destruction, called for by political wickedness and madness, does not come into actual existence because the physical conditions in the sap or in the environment have counterbalanced the internal principle of death — such an accident does not suppress that regularity inherent in the law which I emphasized in the previous part of this essay, and only bears witness to the fact that nations and civilizations are naturally mortal. As I pointed out some moments ago, justice may sometimes, even in a distant future, not actually succeed in preserving a state from ruin and destruction. But justice tends by itself to this preservation; and it is not by virtue of justice, it is by virtue of physical conditions counterbalancing from without the very effects of justice that misfortune will then occur. Machiavellianism and political perversion may sometimes, even in a distant future, not actually break, they may triumph decisively over weak and innocent peoples. But they tend by themselves to self destruction; and it is not by virtue of Machiavellianism and political perversion, it is by virtue of other conditions counterbalancing from without the very effects of these, that success will then occur. . . .

To sum up all that I have stated, I would say First: It suffices to be just in order to gain eternal life; this does not suffice in order to gain battles or immediate political successes.

Second: In order to gain battles or immediate political successes, it is not necessary to be just, it may occasionally be more advantageous to be unjust.

Third: It is necessary, although it is not sufficient, to be just, in order to procure and further the political common good, and the lasting welfare of earthly communities.

The considerations I have developed in my essay are founded on the basic fact that Politics is a branch of Ethics but a branch specifically distinct from the other branches of the same generic stock. One decisive sign of this specificity of Political Ethics in contradistinction to Personal Ethics is that earthly communities are moral as regards their very being and belong entirely to time. Another sign is that political virtues tend to a relatively ultimate end which is the earthly common good, and are only indirectly related to the absolutely ultimate end of man. Hence many features of Political Ethics which I can only allude to here, and which secure its truly realist quality; in such a way that many rules of political life, which the pessimists of Machiavellianism usurp to the benefit of immorality, like the political toleration of certain evils and the recognition of the *fait accompli* (the so-called "statute of limitations") which permits the retention of long ago ill-gotten gains, because new human ties and vital relationships have infused them with new-born rights, are in reality ethically grounded; and in such a way that Political Ethics is able to absorb and digest all the elements of truth contained in Machiavelli, namely, to the extent that power and immediate success are part of politics, but a subordinate part, not the principal part. . . .

Here I emphasize anew what I pointed out at the beginning of this essay. Machiavellianism does not consist of this unhappy lot of particular evil and unjust political deeds which are taking place in fact by virtue of human weakness or wickedness. Machiavellianism is a philosophy of politics, and by essence must make use of evil. What I have discussed is this political philosophy. There will be no end to the occurrence of misdeeds and mistakes as long as humanity endures. To Machiavellianism there can and must be an end.

Let us conclude. Machiavellianism is an illusion, because it rests upon the power of evil, and because, metaphysically, evil as such has no power as a cause of being; practically, evil has no power as a cause of any lasting achievement. As to moral entities like peoples, states, and nations, which do not have any supratemporal destiny, it is within time that their deeds are sanctioned, it is upon earth that the entire charge of failure and nothingness with which is charged every evil action committed by the whole or by its heads, will normally be exhausted. This is a natural, a somewhat physical law in the moral order, although thwarted in some cases by the interference of the manifold other factors at play in human history: as a rule Machiavellianism and political injustice, if they gain immediate success, lead states and nations to misfortune or catastrophe in the long run; in cases where they seem to succeed even in the long run, this is not by virtue of evil and political injustice, but by virtue of some inner principle of misfortune already binding their victim to submission, even if

the latter did not have to face such iniquitous enemies. . . .

If some day absolute Machiavellianism
triumphs over mankind, this will only be
because all kinds of accepted iniquity, moral
weakness, and consent to evil, operating
within a degenerating civilization, will previously have corrupted it, and prepared
ready-made slaves for the lawless man. But
if for the time being absolute Machiavellianism is to be crushed, and I hope so, it will
only be because what remains of Christian
civilization will have been able to oppose it
with the principle of political justice in-
tegrally recognized, and to proclaim to the
world the very end of Machiavellianism.

There is only one determining principle
before which the principle of Machiavellianism finds itself spiritually reduced to
impotence: that is the principle of real and
absolutely unwavering political justice, as
St. Louis understood it. Men will have to
spring up to array against the knighthood
of human degradation the true knighthood
of justice.

THE CONTEMPORARY OUTLOOK

Political Science or Political Satire?

GARRETT MATTINGLY

No recent scholar has produced a more refreshing and challenging reappraisal of *The Prince* than has Garrett Mattingly, professor of modern European history at Columbia University. After study at Harvard, Strasbourg, Paris, and Florence, Mattingly received his Ph.D. from Harvard in 1935, under the direction of Robert Bigelow Merriman. He has returned to Europe on many occasions to continue his research in early diplomatic history. His carefully discerning scholarship and his colorful and lucid style have been combined to produce such unique and definitive studies as *Catherine of Aragon* (1941); *Renaissance Diplomacy* (1955); and *The Armada* (1959).

THE reputation of Niccolò Machiavelli rests on a curious paradox, a paradox so conspicuous and so familiar that we have almost entirely forgotten it. After the collapse of the Florentine republic, which he had served faithfully for fourteen years, Machiavelli relieved the tedium of exile and idleness by taking up his pen. He wrote poems — verse, at least — and tales and plays, including one comedy which is a classic. But mostly he wrote about politics. He was mad about politics. He says in one of his letters that he had to talk about it; he could talk of nothing else. So, in short discourses and political fables, in a history of Florence, in a treatise on the art of war and, notably, in a series of discourses, nominally on the first ten books of Livy, he strove to pass on to his fellow countrymen the fruits of his experience, his reading and his meditation. These are solid works, earnest and thoughtful, often original and provocative. Scholars who have read them usually speak of them with great respect. But not many people ever look at them, and most of those who do have had their curiosity aroused by the one little book which everyone knows: *The Prince.*

The Prince is scarcely more than a pamphlet, a very minor fraction of its author's work, but it overshadows all the rest. Probably no book about politics was ever read more widely. Certainly none has been better known to people who have never read it. Everyone knows that Machiavelli recommended hypocrisy and ingratitude, meanness, cruelty, and treachery as the traits proper to princes. Everyone recognizes "Machiavellian" as an adjective for political conduct that combines diabolical cunning with a ruthless disregard for moral standards. But *The Prince* obsesses historians and political philosophers who know a good deal more about it than that. Its burning prose still casts a lurid glow over the whole landscape of Renaissance Italy: historians who ought to know better call the whole period "the age of Machiavelli" and describe it as if it were chiefly characterized by the kind of behavior on which *The*

From Garrett Mattingly, "Machiavelli's *Prince*: Political Science or Political Satire?" *The American Scholar*, Vol. XXVII (1958), pp. 482–91. Reprinted by permission of Garrett Mattingly and the editors of *The American Scholar*.

Prince dwells; and philosophers, undertaking to describe Machiavelli's political thought, after carefully apprising their readers of the greater weight and complexity of the *Discorsi* and his other writings, end up by choosing half or more of their quotations from one slender volume. But *The Prince* is a short book, and most people remember short books better than long ones. Moreover, *The Prince* is easily Machiavelli's best prose. Its sentences are crisp and pointed, free from the parenthetical explanations and qualifying clauses that punctuate and clog his other political writings. Its prose combines verve and bite with a glittering, deadly polish, like the swordplay of a champion fencer. It uses apt, suggestive images, symbols packed with overtones. For instance: A prince should behave sometimes like a beast, and among beasts he should combine the traits of the lion and the fox. It is studded with epigrams like "A man will forget the death of his father sooner than the loss of his patrimony," epigrams which all seem to come out of some sort of philosophical Grand Guignol and, like the savage ironies of Swift's *Modest Proposal,* are rendered the more spine chilling by the matter-of-fact tone in which they are uttered. And this is where the paradox comes in. Although the method and most of the assumptions of *The Prince* are so much of a piece with Machiavelli's thought that the book could not have been written by anyone else, yet in certain important respects, including some of the most shocking of the epigrams, *The Prince* contradicts everything else Machiavelli ever wrote and everything we know about his life. And everyone who has studied the subject at all has always known this.

The history of Machiavelli's literary reputation underlines the paradox. His other political works were received on publication much as they have been received ever since, respectfully but without undue excitement. However, when *The Prince* was published in 1532, five years after its author's death, it achieved an enormous

succès de scandale. As word of its appalling doctrines spread, all Europe hummed with a chorus of disapproval. For two centuries, to call one's political opponent a disciple of Machiavelli was about the worst thing one could say of him. The cynical immorality of the maxims in *The Prince* horrified even so unscrupulous a young rascal as Frederick the Great of Prussia — or at least he said they did.

Then, as the modern spirit of nationalism dawned, the image of Old Nick began to change. Appropriately enough, it was Herder who first declared that *The Prince* was neither a satire nor an iniquitous guide for political criminals, but an objective study of sixteenth-century Italian politics, offered by a patriot as a service to his country. People began to point out that if Machiavelli recommended behavior of which one could not really approve, he did it for the sake of a united Italy. Some of his counsels were shocking, truly, but only bitter, dangerous medicines would suffice for his corrupt age. So, from being a sort of Byronic diabolist, Machiavelli gradually became a hero, and then a saint of the Italian Risorgimento. Villari's solid volumes proving that Machiavelli was a Florentine patriot, and perhaps even an Italian one, are the chief monument to this nineteenth-century hero-image.

In the twentieth century the image changed again, partly, perhaps, because of difficulties in the nationalist explanation, but mostly, I suspect, because of a change in the prevailing climate of opinion. Kossuth and Garibaldi were being shouldered aside by Darwin and Pasteur, and from being a patriot whose exaggerations were forgivable because of his devotion to torn and trampled Italy, Machiavelli became the passionless, objective scientist, the perfect mirror and analyst of his time. Machiavelli's "objectivity" and "realism" had been praised in the nineteenth century and even earlier by a few people, mostly by philosophers like Herder and Fichte and Hegel, who did not bother to check up on him; but it was Sir Frederick Pollock who, about 1910, first conferred on Machiavelli the proud title of "scientist." As far as I know he has held it to this day, the dissenters being mainly belated exponents of the nationalist-patriot school. In his *Myth of the State* Ernst Cassirer enshrined the current image in an eloquent passage describing Machiavelli watching political behavior and drawing conclusions from it with the passionless detachment of a chemist in a laboratory.

There is a certain superficial plausibility about this view. Since so much of *The Prince* does harmonize with the rest of Machiavelli's thought, and since it is so quotable, the temptation to explain away the discords is hard to resist. And often Machiavelli did say that he wanted to show things as they really are instead of as they ought to be, and often he did try to do so, not only in his state papers, where dispassionate, objective reporting was expected of him, but also in the *Discorsi* and other works in which the literary tradition was different. He tried; he did not always succeed. To insist that republics are always juster, wiser, and more trustworthy than princes, as Machiavelli frequently does in the *Discorsi*, seems a judgment as much charged with subjective emotion as its reverse would be. And, in the year 1520, to dismiss firearms as unimportant in war seems slightly unrealistic even for a cloistered scholar, and rather more so for a man who had been more than a decade the secretary of war of an embattled republic. Yet usually he did try to be objective, and that is why *The Prince* is so serious a stumbling block. The notion that this little book was meant as a serious, scientific treatise on government contradicts everything we know about Machiavelli's life, about his writings, and about the history of his time.

In the first place, this proposition asks us to believe that Niccolò Machiavelli deliberately wrote a handbook meant to help a tyrant rule the once free people of Florence. The Machiavelli were an old Florentine family, noted for their devotion to the republic. In the two centuries before Niccolò was born they had given Florence twelve *gonfalonieri* and fifty-four priors. In the fifteenth century, Niccolò's great-granduncle Girolamo won himself a place in the hearts of the people by suffering imprisonment, torture, exile, and death in defense of their liberty. Another Machiavelli, Francesco, was remembered for a public speech in which he said, "It is freedom that makes cities and their citizens great. This is well known. Tyranny makes only desolation. For tyrants must always fear good citizens and try to exterminate them." Nearly a century later, Niccolò made this assertion one of the central theses of his *Discorsi*, thus prolonging the family tradition in which he was brought up. We know more about his youth now than we did until a few years ago when the diary of Niccolò's father, Bernardo, was found and published. It is not unlike the diaries of many other of the pious, thrifty, hardworking, rather puritanical Florentine petty bourgeoisie who were the backbone of the city's greatness. Bernardo was almost poor and, in those days of Medici domination, without public honors. But he was proud of his family, a firm but affectionate father, anxious to bring up his son to good Latin letters and a devotion to republican principles. Poor as he was, Bernardo had a small library of classics, including, the diary shows, a Livy, which by the time Niccolò was seventeen had to be rebound. To his wife, Bartolomea de'Nelli, the authoress of a number of hymns, *laudi sacre*, Bernardo probably left their son's religious education, but he himself would have seen to it that Niccolò learned the history of his *patria*, how Florence was the citadel of freedom and the guardian of Italian liberty, and the share his own family once had in this glorious heritage.

In the 1470's it was still possible to believe that this heritage was not lost. The constitution of the city was still republican, and though the Medici enjoyed an influence that republicans like Bernardo might regard as sinister, and though the young Medici did not mask their power with the same care their grandfather had used, they were still in form and law just scions of the leading family of a free commonwealth. In fact, as the popular wrath against the Pazzi conspirators proved, most Florentines, particularly the *popolo minuto,* the "little people," still thought of the Medici as the guardians of their liberties both against foreign domination and against the selfish designs of the oligarchs. It was only slowly, in the 1480's, that most Florentines began to realize the attrition of their freedom. When Niccolò was twenty-five they rebelled, and Piero de Medici rode out of the city gates, never to return. Four years later Niccolò Machiavelli was appointed chancellor of the second chancery, and shortly thereafter secretary to the Ten of War. For the next fourteen years he served the Florentine republic with furious, dedicated zeal. He has left the proof of his devotion in the record of his activities and in the state papers in which he spun endless schemes for the defense and aggrandizement of the republic, and constantly preached the same to his superiors. One characteristic quotation is irresistible. The subject is an increase in the defense budget that Machiavelli's master was reluctant to vote. He reminds them with mounting impatience that only strong states are respected by their neighbors and that their neglect of military strength in the recent past has cost them dear, and he ends with anything but detached calm: "Other people learn from the perils of their neighbors, you will not even learn from your own, nor trust yourselves, nor recognize the time you are losing and have lost. I tell you fortune will not alter the sentence it has pronounced unless you alter your behavior. Heaven will not and cannot preserve those bent on their own ruin. But I cannot believe it will come to this, seeing that you are free Florentines and have your liberty in your hands. In the end I believe you will have the same regard for your freedom that men always have who are born free and desire to live free."

Only a man who cared deeply for the independence of his city would use language like this to his employers. But Machiavelli gave an even more impressive proof of his disinterested patriotism. After fourteen years in high office, in a place where the opportunities for dipping into the public purse and into the pockets of his compatriots and of those foreigners he did business with were practically unlimited (among other duties he acted as paymaster-general of the army), Machiavelli retired from public life as poor as when he had entered it. Later he was to refer to this record with pride, but also with a kind of rueful astonishment; and indeed, if this was not a unique feat in his day, it was a very rare one.

For fourteen years Machiavelli served the republic. Then, in 1512, the militia he had counted on so much ran like rabbits at the first sight of the Spanish veterans. There was the bloody sack of Prato, and the republic collapsed before his eyes. The Medici, Cardinal Giovanni and his brother Giuliano, came back behind the Spanish pikes, and while the new government was still unsettled there was a plot to murder them. Two young men named Capponi and Boscoli were arrested. One of them tried to get rid of a paper on which was a short list of names. They were the names of prominent republicans, some of whom had already fled. One was that of Niccolò Machiavelli.

Machiavelli had not fled. Dismissed from office, he still lingered in Florence. He was arrested, imprisoned, and interrogated under torture. Four turns of the rack were usually enough to break a man, body and spirit. Niccolò endured six, and well enough to congratulate himself afterward not just on his survival but on his courage. He admitted nothing, and since nothing could be proved against him, he was released with no further punishment than the loss of his offices, a ruinous fine, and exile to his tiny estate seven miles from the gates of Florence, there to eat his heart out in loneliness and boredom.

Machiavelli emerged from prison in mid-March, 1513. Most people believe that *The*

Prince was finished by December. I suppose it is possible to imagine that a man who has seen his country enslaved, his life's work wrecked and his own career with it, and has, for good measure, been tortured within an inch of his life should thereupon go home and write a book in.ended to teach his enemies the proper way to maintain themselves, writing all the time, remember, with the passionless objectivity of a scientist in a laboratory. It must be possible to imagine such behavior, because Machiavelli scholars do imagine it and accept it without a visible tremor. But it is a little difficult for the ordinary mind to compass.

The difficulty is increased by the fact that this acceptance of tyranny seems to have been a passing phase. Throughout the rest of his life Machiavelli wrote as a republican and moved mainly in republican circles. In 1524 two of his closest friends and patrons, Zanobi Buondelmonti and the poet Luigi Alamanni, were involved in another conspiracy against the Medici and fled. Much later Machiavelli's name was connected with this conspiracy too. The accusation came too late to do him any harm, and nothing was proved. Of course it does not prove anything either that when the Medici were finally driven out again in 1527, Buondelmonti and Alamanni began working at once to bring their old friend back to the service of the restored republic. But the facts do seem to indicate a singularly consistent life, except for one aberration.

The notion that *The Prince* is what it pretends to be, a scientific manual for tyrants, has to contend not only against Machiavelli's life but against his writings, as, of course, everyone who wants to use *The Prince* as a centerpiece in an exposition of Machiavelli's political thought has recognized. Ever since Herder, the standard explanation has been that in the corrupt conditions of sixteenth-century Italy only a prince could create a strong state capable of expansion. The trouble with this is that it was chiefly because they widened their boundaries that Machiavelli preferred republics. In the *Discorsi* he wrote, "We know by experience that states have never signally increased either in territory or in riches except under a free government. The cause is not far to seek, since it is the well-being not of the individuals but of the community which makes the state great, and without question this universal well-being is nowhere secured save in a republic. . . . Popular rule is always better than the rule of princes." This is not just a casual remark. It is the main theme of the *Discorsi* and the basic assumption of all but one of Machiavelli's writings, as it was the basic assumption of his political career.

There is another way in which *The Prince* is a puzzling anomaly. In practically everything else Machiavelli wrote, he displayed the sensitivity and tact of the developed literary temperament. He was delicately aware of the tastes and probable reactions of his public. No one could have written that magnificent satiric soliloquy of Fra Timotheo in *Mandragola,* for instance, who had not an instinctive feeling for the response of an audience. But the effect of the publication of *The Prince* on the first several generations of its readers in Italy (outside of Florence) and in the rest of Europe was shock. It horrified, rebelled, and fascinated like a Medusa's head. A large part of the shock was caused, of course, by the cynical immorality of some of the proposals, but instead of appeasing revulsion and insinuating his new proposals as delicately as possible, Machiavelli seems to delight in intensifying the shock and deliberately employing devices to heighten it. Of these not the least effective is the way *The Prince* imitates, almost parodies, one of the best known and most respected literary forms of the three preceding centuries, the handbook of advice to princes. This literary type was enormously popular. Its exemplars ran into the hundreds of titles of which a few, like St. Thomas' *De Regno* and Erasmus' *Institutio principis christiani* are not quite unknown today. In some ways, Machiavelli's little treatise was just like all the other "Mirrors of Princes"; in other ways it was a diabolical burlesque of all of them, like a political Black Mass.

The shock was intensified again because Machiavelli deliberately addressed himself primarily to princes who have newly acquired their principalities and do not owe them either to inheritance or to the free choice of their countrymen. The short and ugly word for this kind of prince is "tyrant." Machiavelli never quite uses the word except in illustrations from classical antiquity, but he seems to delight in dancing all around it until even the dullest of his readers could not mistake his meaning. Opinions about the relative merits of republics and monarchies varied during the Renaissance, depending mainly upon where one lived, but about tyrants there was only one opinion. Cristoforo Landino, Lorenzo the Magnificent's teacher and client, stated the usual view in his commentary on Dante, written when Niccolò Machiavelli was a child. When he came to comment on Brutus and Cassius in the lowest circle of hell, Landino wrote: "Surely it was extraordinary cruelty to inflict such severe punishment on those who faced death to deliver their country from slavery, a deed for which, if they had been Christians, they would have merited the most honored seats in the highest heaven. If we consult the laws of any well-constituted republic, we shall find them to decree no greater reward to anyone than to the man who kills the tyrant." So said the Italian Renaissance with almost unanimous voice. If Machiavelli's friends were meant to read the manuscript of *The Prince* and if they took it at face value — an objective study of how to be a successful tyrant offered as advice to a member of the species — they can hardly have failed to be deeply shocked. And if the manuscript was meant for the eye of young Giuliano de Medici alone, he can hardly have been pleased to find it blandly assumed that he was one of a class of whom his father's tutor had written that the highest duty of a good citizen was to kill them.

The literary fame of *The Prince* is due, precisely, to its shocking quality, so if the book was seriously meant as a scientific manual, it owes its literary reputation to an artistic blunder. And if it was meant for a Medici prince, it has at its core an even more inexplicable piece of tactlessness. For to the Medici prince, "to a new prince established by fortune and the arms of others," Machiavelli offers Cesare Borgia as a model. There was just enough truth to the suggestion that Giuliano de Medici owed his principate "to the arms of others" — after all, it was the Spanish troops who overthrew the republic as it was French troops who established Cesare in the Romagna — to be wounding. There was just enough cogency in the comparison between the duke of Valentinois, a pope's son, and the duke of Nemours, a pope's brother, to make it stick. These things merely heightened the affront. A Medici, of a family as old and as illustrious as any in Florence, a man whose great-grandfather, grandfather, and father had each in turn been acknowledged the first citizen of the republic and who now aspired to no more than to carry on their tradition (or so he said) was being advised to emulate a foreigner, a Spaniard, a bastard, convicted, in the court of public opinion anyway, of fratricide, incest, and a long role of abominable crimes, a man specially hated in Tuscany for treachery and extortion and for the gross misconduct of his troops on neutral Florentine soil, and a man, to boot, who as a prince had been a notorious and spectacular failure.

This almost forgotten fact lies at the heart of the mystery of *The Prince*. We remember what Machiavelli wrote about Cesare in his most famous work, and we forget what Cesare was. But in 1513 most Italians would not have forgotten the events of 1503, and unless we assume that Machiavelli himself had forgotten what he himself had reported ten or eleven years before, we can scarcely believe that his commendation of the Borgia was seriously meant. If we take *The Prince* as an objective, scientific description of political reality, we must face contradiction not only by what we know of Machiavelli's political career, of his usual opinions and of his literary skill, but also by the facts of history as reported by, among others, Machiavelli himself.

Let us take just a few instances, the crucial ones. Relying on assertions in Chapter Seven of *The Prince,* most historians in the past hundred years have written as if the Borgia had restored peace and order in the Romagna, unified its government and won the allegiance of its inhabitants. Part of the time this must have been going on, Machiavelli was an envoy in the duke's camp. Although he does warn the signory repeatedly that Valentino is a formidable ruffian, daring, unscrupulous, and of unlimited ambition, he never mentions these statesmanlike achievements — nor do any of the other reports from observers in the area, Spanish, French, Venetian, Sienese; nor do any other contemporary sources. All the indications are quite contrary. The most probing recent study of Valentino's career, Gabriele Pepe's *La Politica dei Borgia,* sums the matter up by saying that the duke did nothing to end factional strife and anarchy in the Romagna; he merely superimposed the brutal rule of his Spanish captains on top of it.

We can make a concrete check on a related instance. After saying in Chapter Thirteen that the duke had used first French troops, then mercenaries under *condottieri* captains and then his own men, Machiavelli comments, "He was never esteemed more highly than when everyone saw that he was complete master of his own forces." But in the *Legazione,* Machiavelli never once refers to the military capacity of the duke or praises the courage or discipline of his army. Instead, as late as December 14, 1502, he writes from Imola of the troops under Cesare's own command: "They have devoured everything here except the stones . . . here in the Romagna they are behaving just as they did in Tuscany last year [of their passage then, Landucci had noted in his diary that none of the foreign armies that had crossed Tuscany in the past seven years had behaved

so abominably as these Italians under the papal banner] and they show no more discipline and no less confusion than they did then." There is no subsequent indication that Machiavelli ever changed his mind.

Nowhere is *The Prince* more at odds with the facts of history or with Machiavelli's own previous judgments than in the famous concluding passage of Chapter Seven on which any favorable opinion of Cesare's statecraft must be based. The passage in *The Prince* reads: "On the day Pope Julius II was elected, the Duke told me that he had thought of everything that might happen on the death of his father and provided for everything except that when his father died he himself would be at death's door . . . only the shortness of the life of Alexander and his own sickness frustrated his designs. Therefore he who wants to make sure of a new principality . . . cannot find a better model than the actions of this man." Could Machiavelli have believed this in 1513? He certainly did not believe it in 1503. He did not even record then that Cesare ever said anything of the sort; and though it would not be unlike some of the duke's whimperings, he could not have said it on the day of Julius II's election, when he was boasting to everyone that the new pope would obey him. In any case, Machiavelli would have believed what, in *The Prince,* he said the duke said, as little as he believed the bluster that, in 1503, he actually reported. By November of 1503, nobody could have believed it. In fact, even in August, when Alexander VI died, at the age of seventy-two after a papacy of eleven years (not such a short life and not such a short reign), most people in Rome, including all of the ambassadors whose reports survive and most of the cardinals with whom they had talked, felt sure Cesare was finished. He had always ridden on his father's shoulders, and he was hated, feared, and despised even by most of the faction who had stood by the old pope. No one trusted him, and there was no one he could trust. No pope would dare support him, and without papal support his principate was built on quicksand. He had never, in fact, faced this eventual predicament, and he did not face it when it arose. It is true that he was ill in August with a bout of malaria, but not too ill to stall the election and then maneuver the choice of the old and ailing Pius III, thus delaying an unavoidable doom. Julius II was not elected until November. In all those months and even after the election, Italy was treated through the eyes of its ambassadors to the spectacle of the terrible Borgia duke writhing in an agony of indecision, now about to go to Genoa to raise money, now ready to start for an interview with the king of France, now on the point of leading his troops back to the Romagna, but in fact hovering about the curia, plucking the sleeves of cardinals and bowing and smiling to envoys he used to bully, sometimes swaggering through the streets with the powerful armed guard he felt he needed to protect him from the vengeance of the Orsini, sometimes shaking beneath bedclothes with what might have been fever and might have been funk. We catch a glimpse of him at midnight in the chamber of Guidobaldo de Montrefeltre, the duke of Urbino, who had been newly restored to his former estates by the loyalty of his subjects, and to his former rank of *gonfaloniere* of the church by the new pope. There Cesare kneels on the floor, sobbing in pure terror, begging the old friend whom he had betrayed and robbed, with incredible meanness, not just of his duchy, but of his books and his antique medals, not to kill him, please not to kill him, to leave him at least his life, until Guidobaldo, beyond any feeling about this curious monster, says he does not wish to kill him; he only wishes him to go away.

Shortly thereafter Cesare slinks off to Naples and imprisonment, followed by the scornful laughter of Italy. For nothing is more absurd than the great straw-stuffed giants of carnival, and when such a giant has for a season frightened all Italy, the laughter is that much the louder. Machia-

velli was one of the ambassadors in Rome. He knew all this as well as anyone. One can read in dispatches his growing impatience with the duke, his growing contempt for Cesare's wild talk, aimless shifts of plan, alternate blustering and whining. "The duke, who never kept faith with anyone," he wrote, "is now obliged to rely on the faith of others." And later, "The duke, who never showed mercy, now finds mercy his only hope." Later in his historical poem, *Decennali*, Machiavelli made his distaste for the Borgia clear enough. Did he really mean to propose him in 1513 as a model prince? Was he writing as a friend of tyrants or as a dispassionate scientific observer when he said he did?

There is, of course, an alternative view, never predominant and now hopelessly old-fashioned, but one that was held by some quite respectable people. The earliest explicit statement of it I know comes from Alberico Gentili, an Italian who lectured on the civil law at Oxford in the reign of Elizabeth I. Speaking of his fellow countryman, Gentili wrote, in part: "He has been much calumniated and deserves our sympathy. He was, indeed, a praiser of democracy (*Democratiae laudator*) and its most zealous champion. Born, educated, and honored with office in a republic, he was a supreme foe of tyrants. It was his purpose not to instruct tyrants but to reveal their secret machinations, stripping them bare before their suffering people . . . he aimed to instruct [those] people under the pretext of instructing the prince, hoping that thus his teaching might be tolerated." Toward the end of the seventeenth century, Baruch Spinoza, without, I think, ever having read Gentili, expressed a similar opinion, and nearly a hundred years later Jean Jacques Rousseau concurred. In the course of those centuries before violent nationalism had blurred men's vision, enough writers must have identified *The Prince* as a satire so that Herder felt compelled to begin his defense by indignantly repudiating this view.

Perhaps nobody should be rash enough

today to call *The Prince* a satire, not in the teeth of all the learned opinion to the contrary. But when one comes to think of it, what excellent sense the idea makes! However you define "satire" — and I understand that critics are still without a thoroughly satisfactory definition — it must include the intention to denounce, expose, or deride someone or something, and it is to be distinguished from mere didactic condemnation and invective (when it can be distinguished at all) by the employment of such devices as irony, sarcasm, and ridicule. It need not be provocative of laughter; I doubt whether many people ever laughed or even smiled at the adventures of Gulliver among the Yahoos. And though satire admits of, and in fact always employs, exaggeration and overemphasis, the author, to be effective, must not appear to be, and in fact need not be, conscious that this is so. When Dryden wrote, "The rest to some faint meaning make pretense / But Shadwell never deviates into sense," he may have been conscious of some overstatement, but he was conveying his considered criticism of Shadwell's poetry. And when Pope called "Lord Fanny" "this painted child of dirt that stinks and stings," the language may be violent, but who can doubt that this is how Pope felt? Indeed the satirist seems to put forth his greatest powers chiefly when goaded by anger, hatred, and savage indignation. If Machiavelli wrote *The Prince* out of the fullness of these emotions rather than out of the dispassionate curiosity of the scientist or out of a base willingness to toady to the destroyers of his country's liberty, then one can understand why the sentences crack like a whip, why the words bite and burn like acid, and why the whole style had a density and impact unique among his writings.

To read *The Prince* as satire not only clears up puzzles and resolves contradictions; it gives a new dimension and meaning to passages unremarkable before. Take the place in the dedication that runs "just as those who paint landscapes must seat themselves below in the plains to see the moun-

tains, and high in the mountains to see the plains, so to understand the nature of the people one must be a prince, and to understand the nature of a prince, one must be one of the people." In the usual view, this is a mere rhetorical flourish, but the irony, once sought, is easy to discover, for Machiavelli, in fact, takes both positions. The people can only see the prince as, by nature and necessity, false, cruel, mean, and hypocritical. The prince, from his lofty but precarious perch, dare not see the people as other than they are described in Chapter Seventeen: "ungrateful, fickle, treacherous, cowardly, and greedy. As long as you succeed they are yours entirely. They will offer you their blood, property, lives, and children when you do not need them. When you do need them, they will turn against you." Probably Machiavelli really believed that this, or something like it, happened to the human nature of a tyrant and his subjects. But the view, like its expression, is something less than objective and dispassionate, and the only lesson it has for princes would seem to be: "Run for your life!"

Considering the brevity of the book, the number of times its princely reader is reminded, as in the passage just quoted, that his people will overthrow him at last is quite remarkable. Cities ruled in the past by princes easily accustom themselves to a change of master, Machiavelli says in Chapter Five, but "in republics there is more vitality, greater hatred, and more desire for vengeance. They cannot forget their lost liberty, so that the safest way is to destroy them — or to live there." He does not say what makes that safe. And most notably, with savage irony, "the duke [Borgia] was so able and laid such firm foundations . . . that the Romagna [after Alexander VI's death] waited for him more than a month." This is as much as to put Leo X's brother on notice that without papal support he can expect short shrift. If the Romagna, accustomed to tyranny, waited only a month before it rose in revolt, how long will Florence wait? Tactlessness like this is unintelligible unless it is deliberate, unless these are not pedantic blunders but sarcastic ironies, taunts flung at the Medici, incitements to the Florentines.

Only in a satire can one understand the choice of Cesare Borgia as the model prince. The common people of Tuscany could not have had what they could expect of a prince's rule made clearer than by the example of this bloodstained buffoon whose vices, crimes, and follies had been the scandal of Italy, and the conduct of whose brutal, undisciplined troops had so infuriated the Tuscans that when another band of them crossed their frontier, the peasants fell upon them and tore them to pieces. The Florentine aristocrats on whom Giovanni and cousin Giulio were relying to bridge the transition to despotism would have shared the people's revulsion to Cesare, and they may have been rendered somewhat more thoughtful by the logic of the assumption that nobles were more dangerous to a tyrant than commoners and should be dealt with as Cesare had dealt with the petty lords of the Romagna. Moreover, they could scarcely have avoided noticing the advice to use some faithful servant to terrorize the rest, and then to sacrifice him to escape the obloquy of his conduct, as Cesare had sacrificed Captain Ramiro. As for the gentle, mild-mannered, indolent Giuliano de Medici himself, he was the last man to be attracted by the notion of imitating the Borgia. He wanted no more than to occupy the same social position in Florence that his magnificent father had held, and not even that if it was too much trouble. Besides, in the days of the family's misfortunes, Giuliano had found shelter and hospitality at the court of Guidobaldo de Montrefeltre. Giuliano lived at Urbino for many years (there is a rather charming picture of him there in Castiglione's *Il Cortegiano*), and all his life he cherished deep gratitude and a strong affection for Duke Guidobaldo. He must have felt, then, a special loathing for the foreign ruffian who had betrayed and plun-

dered his patron, and Machiavelli must have known that he did. Only a wish to draw the most odious comparison possible, only a compulsion to wound and insult, could have led Machiavelli to select the Borgia as the prime exemplar in his "Mirror of Princes."

There is one last famous passage that reads differently if we accept *The Prince* as satire. On any other hypothesis, the final exhortation to free Italy from the barbarians sounds at best like empty rhetoric, at worst like calculating but stupid flattery. Who could really believe that the lazy, insipid Giuliano or his petty, vicious successor were the liberators Italy awaited? But if we have heard the mordant irony and sarcasm of the preceding chapters and detected the overtones of hatred and despair, then this last chapter will be charged with an irony turned inward, the bitter mockery of misdirected optimism. For before the Florentine republic had been gored to death by Spanish pikes, Machiavelli had believed, as he was to believe again, that a free Florentine republic could play the liberator's role. Perhaps, since he was all his life a passionate idealist, blind to reality when his desires were strong, Machiavelli may not have given up that wild hope even when he wrote *The Prince*. If he had not, then the verses at the end take on a new meaning, clearer perhaps to his contemporaries than they can be to us.

Virtù contro a furore
Prenderà l'arme, e fia il combatter corto;
Chè l'antico valore
Nell'italici cor non è ancor morto.

The antique valor Petrarch appealed to was, after all, that of republican Rome. Perhaps that first sharp combat was not to be against the barbarians.

However that may be, we must agree that if *The Prince* was meant as a satire, as a taunt and challenge to the Medici and a tocsin to the people of Florence, then it must have been recognized as such by the Florentine literati and by the Medici themselves. If so we have the solution to two minor puzzles connected with this puzzling book. A rasher ruling family than the Medici might have answered the challenge by another round of torture and imprisonment or by a quiet six inches of steel under the fifth rib. But brother Giovanni and brother Giovanni's familiar spirit, cousin Giulio, though in fact they were aiming at exactly the kind of despotism that Machiavelli predicted, hoped to achieve it with a minimum of trouble by preserving for the time being the forms of the republic. It would not do, by punishing the author, to admit the pertinence of his satire. So the Medici did nothing. But they were not a stupid family, and they cannot have been very pleased. This would explain some puzzling things: why, for example, the ardent republicans among Machiavelli's friends, like Zanobi Buondelmonti, were not alienated by *The Prince*, and why the former republicans in Medici service among his correspondents, like Vettori, for instance, refer to it so seldom and with such muffled embarrassment. It would also explain why, among all the manuscripts of *The Prince* dating from Machiavelli's lifetime (and it seems to have had a considerable circulation and to have been multiplied by professional copyists), we have never found the copy which should have had the best chance of preservation — I mean that copy, beautifully lettered on vellum and richly bound, presented with its dedication to the Medici prince. Not only is it absent from the Laurentian library now, there is no trace that it was ever there. There is no evidence that it ever existed. Probably Machiavelli figured that the joke was not worth the extra expense.

SUGGESTIONS FOR ADDITIONAL READING

Only the recent and most available books and articles are mentioned in this bibliography, which represents of course only a fraction of the vast Machiavelli literature. Of the more general studies of Machiavelli's life and times, the student can still find the works of Villari and Tommasini useful, but for most aspects of this subject the newer *Vita di Niccolò Machiavelli* (Rome, 1954) by Roberto Ridolfi, is much more reliable, penetrating, and also more refreshingly written. In English the selection is poor, but Dorothy Erskine Muir's *Machiavelli and His Times* (London, 1936) is a useful book with some very interesting chapters on his literary career, and Jeffrey Pulver's sympathetic appraisal in *Machiavelli, the Man, his Work and his Times* (London, 1937) is also well worth the reading. Giuseppe Prezzolini's *Nicolo Machiavelli the Florentine,* translated by Ralph Roeder (New York, 1928) is a fast-moving but rather superficial survey of his life, as is Valeriu Marcu's *Accent on Power: The Life and Times of Machiavelli,* translated by Richard Winston (New York, 1939). A more reliable, though very brief, sketch of Machiavelli's life is provided in Ferdinand Schevill's *Six Historians* (Chicago, 1956), pp. 61–91, and a most intriguing but somewhat fanciful one in Ralph Roeder's *Man of the Renaissance* (New York, 1933), chapters 2 and 3, available also in paperback (Meridian Books, 1958). Some useful new insights into Machiavelli's life are furnished by Marcel Brion in his *Machiavel: génie & destinée* (Paris, 1948), and Georges Mounin, *Machiavel* (Paris, 1957). Orestes Ferrara's *Maquiavelo: la vida, las obras, la fama* (Madrid, 1943) emphasizes Machiavelli's public life as a motivation in his thought and writings, and has some valuable chapters on his diplomatic missions. The following articles deal in more detail with specific aspects of his life: Simon Harcourt-Smith, "Machiavelli," *History Today,* VI (1956), 45–53; Felix Gilbert's noteworthy "Machiavelli: The Renaissance of the Art of War," in Edward Mead Earle (ed.), *The Makers of Modern Strategy* (Princeton, 1944); Allan H. Gilbert, "Machiavelli on Fire Weapons," *Italica,* XXIII (1946), 275–86; and Judith Janoska-Bendl, "Niccolò Machiavelli: Politik ohne Ideologie," *Archiv für Kulturgeschichte,* XL (1958), 315–45, which treats Machiavelli as a product of the crisis period of the Italian Renaissance. The only book which studies Machiavelli as a diplomat is Eugenio Dupré Thesseider's *Niccolò Machiavelli diplomatico* (Milan, 1948).

The variety and complexity of Machiavelli's thought has been the subject of many recent scholarly monographs. An outstanding example is Luigi Russo's *Machiavelli,* 4th ed. (Bari, 1957), which also contains a summary of Machiavelli criticism. Gennaro Sasso, in his *Niccolò Machiavelli: storia del suo pensiero politico* (Naples, 1958), carefully examines Machiavelli's political thought, and in so doing has produced one of the best analyses of the influences of the times upon the evolution of his ideas. Other very worthwhile studies of this subject are Augustin Renaudet's *Machiavel: étude d'histoire des doctrines politiques* (Paris, 1942), an important work by a great scholar; J. H. Whitfield's *Machiavelli* (Oxford, 1947), a sympathetic and penetrating study; and Harold J. Laski's chapter "Machiavelli and the Present Time," in *The Dangers of Obedience and Other Essays* (New York, 1930). Of the many articles on particular aspects of Machiavelli's thought, the following are most useful: Edward M. Burns, "The Liberalism of Machiavelli," *Antioch Review,* VIII (1948), 121–30; Aldo Scaglione, "Machiavelli the Scientist?" *Symposium,* X (1956), 243–50; chapter II, "Machiavelli: the Science of Power," of James Burnham's *The Machiavellians: Defenders of Free-*

dom (New York, 1943); and Felix Gilbert's "Political Thought of the Renaissance and Reformation," *Huntington Library Quarterly*, IV (1941), 443–68. Most college surveys of political theory also contain a chapter on the political thought of Machiavelli.

For a more specific analysis of Machiavelli's concept of the State and its place in society, Francesco Ercole's works are of great importance. In addition to numerous articles on the subject, his book *La politica di Machiavelli* (Rome, 1926) summarizes Ercole's essential agreement with what he calls Machiavelli's belief in the absolute supremacy of the state and the surrender of all private and personal interests to it. Students can also find profit in a perusal of Gerhard Ritter's *The Corrupting Influence of Power* (London, 1952), a recent translation of his very stimulating and perceptive *Machtstaat und Utopie*, which contrasts Machiavelli's theory of the state with that of Sir Thomas More. Somewhat older but similarly suggestive is Giuseppe Toffanin's *Machiavelli e il tacitismo* (Padua, 1921), which approaches Machiavelli's reliance upon absolutism from the viewpoint of Tacitus's concept of the Roman state. See also Germán Arciniegas, "Savonarola, Machiavelli, and Guido Antonio Vespucci: Totalitarian and Democrat 500 Years Ago," *Political Science Quarterly*, LXIX (1954), 184–201, which maintains that modern totalitarianism is a blending of Machiavelli's theories and Savonarola's techniques of rabble rousing.

The problem of semantics in Machiavelli's writings has opened another large avenue of investigation. For revealing discussions of his use of the word "state," see J. H. Whitfield, "The Politics of Machiavelli," *Modern Language Review*, L (1955), 433–43; and especially J. H. Hexter, "*Il principe* and *lo stato*," *Studies in the Renaissance*, IV (1957), 113–38. The whole problem of language in Machiavelli, including his use of the word "state," is the subject of Fredi Chiappelli's painstaking

Studi sul linguaggio del Machiavelli (Florence, 1952). The use of other terms is examined in J. H. Whitfield, "On Machiavelli's Use of 'Ordini'," *Italian Studies*, X (1955), 19–39; Felix Gilbert's short "On Machiavelli's Idea of Virtù," *Renaissance News*, IV (1951), 53–55 (see also Vol. V, 1952, pp. 21–23); and Hans de Vries, *Essai sur la terminologie constitutionelle chez Machiavel* (The Hague, 1957), with text in French, English, German, and Dutch.

The problem of *The Prince* and its relationship to the humanist writers of the fourteenth-fifteenth centuries, and particularly to their "Mirror of Prince" literature, is the subject of Allan H. Gilbert's *Machiavelli's Prince and Its Forerunners: The Prince as a Typical Book de Regimine Principum* (Durham, 1938), and also of Felix Gilbert's "The Humanist Concept of the Prince and *The Prince* of Machiavelli," *Journal of Modern History*, XI (1939), 449–83, although they each arrive at somewhat different conclusions. Other suggestive studies of *The Prince* are: Eric Voegelin, "Machiavelli's Prince: Background and Formation," *Review of Politics*, XIII (1951), 142–68; J. H. Whitfield, "Savonarola and the Purpose of the Prince," *Modern Language Review*, XLIV (1949), 44–59; Leo Strauss, "Machiavelli's Intention: 'The Prince'," *American Political Science Review*, LI (1957), 13–40, which also forms a chapter of his recent critique, *Thoughts on Machiavelli* (Glencoe, Ill., 1958); and Gennaro Sasso, "Sul VII capitolo del Principe," *Rivista Storica Italiana*, LXIV (1952), 177–207, which examines Machiavelli's view of *fortuna* in the acquisition of power and territory. For reading *The Prince* itself in English, students will find the Mentor edition, 1958 (translated by Luigi Ricci and introduced by Christian Gauss), to be quite handy. An excellent two-volume edition of *The Discourses*, with a detailed introduction and copious notes, has been translated and published by Leslie J. Walker, S.J. (New Haven, 1950). In the near future a new

English edition of Machiavelli's works, translated by Allan H. Gilbert, is to be published by Duke University Press. This welcome 3-volume edition will include *The Prince, Discourses, Life of Castruccio, The Art of War, History of Florence,* and several others.

On the unsolved problem of the composition of *The Prince* and *The Discourses* see Federico Chabod, "Sulla composizione di 'Il Principe' di Niccolò Machiavelli," *Archivum Romanicum,* XI (1927), 330–83, who maintains that *The Prince* was written between July and December of 1513 *after* Machiavelli had begun the first book of *The Discourses;* Felix Gilbert, "The Structure and Composition of Machiavelli's Discorsi," *Journal of the History of Ideas,* XIV (1953), 136–56, who holds that Machiavelli's remark in *The Prince,* that he was refraining from discussing republics because he had already discussed them elsewhere, refers not to *The Discourses,* since that was not yet begun, but to some lost manuscript dealing specifically with republics; and Hans Baron, "The 'Principe' and the Puzzle of the Date of the 'Discorsi'," *Bibliothèque d'Humanisme et Renaissance,* XVIII (1956), 405–28, who suggests that the above remark in *The Prince* was added later, after *The Discourses* was completed. See also J. H. Hexter, "Seyssel, Machiavelli, and Polybius VI: the Mystery of the Missing Translation," *Studies in the Renaissance,* III (1956), 75–96, which complicates the controversy by showing that much of Book I of *The Discourses,* particularly the things about republics, could have been taken from Book VI of Polybius — but not until after 1515! J. H. Whitfield has challenged these last views in his recent article, "Gilbert, Hexter, and Baron," *Italian Studies,* XIII (1958), 21–46; and Gennaro Sasso has defended Chabod's position in his own "Machiavelli e la teoria dell' anacyclo-sis," *Rivista Storica Italiana,* LXX (1958), 333–75.

The subject of the impact of Machiavelli on other people and countries has an enormous bibliography, but only a few examples can be included here. Some of the most interesting and pointed of these are: T. M. Parker, "Was Thomas Cromwell a Machiavellian?" *Journal of Ecclesiastical History,* I (1950), 63–75; Fernando Scorretti, *Machiavel et les Suisses* (Neuchâtel, 1942); Donald Bleznick, "Spanish Reactions to Machiavelli in the 16th and 17th Centuries," *Journal of the History of Ideas,* XIX (1958), 542–50; G. Cardascia, "Machiavel et Jean Bodin," *Bibliothèque d'Humanisme et Renaissance,* III (1943), 129–67; Mario Praz, *Machiavelli and the Elizabethans* (London, 1928), also in his *The Flaming Heart* (Anchor paperbacks, 1958), chap. 2, pp. 90–146; W. A. Armstrong, "The Influence of Seneca and Machiavelli on the Elizabethan Tyrant," *Review of English Studies,* XXIV (1948), 19–35; George L. Mosse, "The Assimilation of Machiavelli in English Thought," *Huntington Library Quarterly,* XVIII (1954), 215–26; Carlo Curcio, *Machiavelli nel Risorgimento* (Milan, 1953); Albert Cherel, *La pensée de Machiavel en France* (Paris, 1935); and Giuseppe Prezzolini, *Machiavelli anticristo* (Rome, 1954), which summarizes Machiavelli's influence in Europe, Russia, and the United States from the sixteenth century to the present. Finally, some very useful insights can also be gained from Felix Gilbert's "Machiavelli and Guiccardini," *Journal of the Warburg Institute,* II (1939), 263–66; J. H. Whitfield's "Machiavelli and Castruccio," *Italian Studies,* VIII (1953), 1–28; and Renzo Sereno's recent re-evaluation of Machiavelli's relations with Cesare Borgia, "A Falsification by Machiavelli," *Renaissance News,* XII (1959), 159–67.